Workbook

For

Tim Ferriss'

The 4-Hour Body

Knowledge Press

This is an unofficial workbook for Tim Ferriss' "The 4-Hour Body: An Uncommon Guide to Rapid Fat-Loss, Incredible Sex, and Becoming Superhuman" designed to enhance your reading and learning. You can get the original book using the QR code with your smartphone or tablet.

Table of Contents

How To Use This Book

How To Use This Guide

"The 4-Hour Body" by Timothy Ferriss serves as a comprehensive guide for optimizing various aspects of life. If you're pressed for time, this workbook is ideal for you. Here's a practical approach to using this guide effectively:

1. Grasp Key Ideas: Familiarize yourself with the summary's core principles, such as the Minimal Effective Dose (MED) concept, aiming for maximum results with minimal effort.

2. Figure Out What to Focus On: Determine which aspects of your life you want to improve, be it fat loss, strength training, sleep, or performance enhancement.

3. Focus on Actionable Insights: Concentrate on a few actionable tips that align with your goals, like specific diet recommendations or exercise routines for desired outcomes.

4. Experiment and Personalize: Embrace Ferriss's encouragement for self-experimentation, customizing recommendations to suit your preferences and lifestyle.

5. Track Progress: Monitor changes in your body, energy levels, and well-being, adjusting your approach based on the observed responses.

6. Embrace Unconventionality: Be open-minded to Ferriss's unconventional ideas, which can potentially lead to amazing changes.

These steps can help you apply the principles and strategies from "The 4-Hour Body" to hopefully change and improve your life in a dramatic way.

Introduction

Timothy Ferriss' groundbreaking book, "The 4-Hour Body," was published in 2010 defies norms by presenting unconventional health and fitness methods aimed at achieving exceptional results in minimal time.

This summary uncovers Ferriss's innovative concepts, starting with the Slow-Carb Diet for sustainable weight loss and other dietary habits. It details fat loss strategies, including minimalistic strength training, cold exposure, and insights on supplements.

For muscle gain, Ferriss emphasizes compound exercises, efficient workouts, and hormonal impact.

Sleep optimization techniques, injury recovery, and posture improvement methods are also explored.

Overall, Ferriss challenges norms and encourages experimentation while also advising consultations with healthcare professionals when necessary.

Chapter 1: Revelation of a New Way

Diary of a Madman

The 4-Hour Body (4HB) is an unconventional guide made by an unexpected experimentalist, Timothy Ferriss. This handbook will teach you how to reduce your body fat in two weeks, increase insulin sensitivity, change your muscle fiber type, and more. **Changing small habits will produce huge outcomes.** Ferriss has navigated through various worlds just to answer his questions and produce the results that he wanted. His self-proclaimed "obsession" is the exact amount of passion needed to produce the out-of-this-world solutions contained in this book (pg. 24)

The Unintentional Dark Horse

Ferriss credits his answers to his ability to be "outside the system" (pg. 28). By not having a PhD or any mandatory publications to produce, he has had the freedom to experiment as he likes. By being on the inside of the medical world without restraints, Ferriss has mastered the ability to spot clouded clinical trials and how consumers can be deceived. The 4-Hour Body will **teach readers how to spot poor science and bad advice** (pg. 27).

A Laboratory of One / The Future's Already Here

Current research breakthroughs are 10-20 years late because of the long process of getting that information to the general public.

Why wait for late research when you can make the change for yourself today?

Multiple sources are accessible to everyone. You can collect personal data for whatever your desired health objective is. This book does not recommend implementing harmful strategies or substances but rather proven procedures that enhance health.

The 80/20 Principle: From Wall Street to the Human Machine

The *4HB* is a method that suggests that only 2.5% of effort is needed to achieve 95% of the desired goal. The rare 1% of people who achieve chiseled physiques and god-like strength are those the other 99% of people compare themselves to.

People are always seeking to invest the least amount of time but gain massive rewards.

This book is a promise to the majority of the population that they can also achieve their dream body by following the tips and steps Ferriss has devised.

How to Use This Book - Five Rules

Ferriss is well aware of his experiments and the science behind each one. With that, he has created **"Five Rules" for readers to keep in mind** when implementing this book's contents.

1. **Pick and choose what to read:** Do not read this book in one sitting. For someone to truly reinvent themselves, they must pick chapters that relate to them and slowly implement it into their personal lives.

2. **Do not be overwhelmed by science**: Not all people have a background in science. Some of this book's "Geek's Advantage" content can become lost in translation. It is not required for readers to become knowledgeable on this extra science but is encouraged if there's an interest.

3. **Be skeptical**: It's always good to question new information. However, Ferriss is fully confident that everything he states in this book is "100% reliable" and does work.

4. **Don't let the skepticism stop you from trying**: Everything is worth a try when done safely. Try these new techniques because you want to choose the best option for yourself, not because you need an excuse to stay in your comfort zone.

5. **Enjoy it**: This is most likely new information and that in itself is exciting to explore. The author experienced many peculiar events to obtain the findings that he did. These stories are eye-opening and light-hearted, so enjoy reading this content less as a book and more as a journey.

The Billionaire Productivity Secret and the Experimental Lifestyle

Most, if not all, people struggle at some point with their productivity levels. It's a common human quality.

One of the most-asked questions of all time is: "How can I be more productive?"

Ferriss insists that **this book is a call for change in lifestyle.** Anybody can read The 4-Hour Body and find positive changes within themselves. The author spent years formulating this book specifically to help those who have been distressed because of body image, nutrition struggles, and unsuccessful attempts to reach their health goals.

Key Takeaways

- Small steps will accumulate into big changes; you just need patience and consistency.
- Don't wait for others to tell you what you can and can't do to improve your health.
- Take multiple opinions into account and choose the best options for yourself.
- Try new things. Just because you might not know the science behind a strategy doesn't mean you should be scared of it.
- Focus on one or two goals at a time. Trying to change anymore at one time will become overwhelming.

Over to You

1. Take some time to fill in the graph with a list of health-related goals that you're proud of yourself for achieving currently. These can be big goals, such as being consistent at the gym, or small things, like making sure to eat a fruit or vegetable every day. This list should be full of positive small habits that make you feel good about yourself.

Positive Health Habits
1.
2.
3.
4.
5.
6.
7.
8.

2. Once you recognize the successful things you do for yourself, you can plan out how to elevate them further. Complete this next graph with only a few health goals you have for yourself. Again, they can be something big, like losing 50 pounds ,or something small, like learning how to cook better foods. When you have found five goals for yourself, rank them in order from most important to least important in the second table.

Health Goals
1.
2.
3.
4.
5.

Health Goals In Order of Importance
1.
2.
3.
4.
5.

3. The next exercise is to look over the different sections and types of information included in the 4HB. Below is a guideline to some of the more popular goals within the book and the order in how to read them. It is important to break up each section before diving head-first and becoming lost in the information.

Rapid Fat-Loss
All chapters in "Fundamentals"
All chapters in "Ground Zero"
"The Slow-Carb Diet I and II"
"Building the Perfect Posterior"

Rapid Muscle Gain
All chapters in "Fundamentals"
All chapters in "Ground Zero"
"From Geek to Freak"
"Occam's Protocol I and II"

Rapid Strength Gain
All chapters in "Fundamentals"

All chapters in "Ground Zero"
"Effortless Superhuman" (pure strength, little mass gain)
"Pre-Hab: Injury-Proofing the Body"

Rapid Sense of Total Well-Being
All chapters in "Fundamentals"
All chapters in "Ground Zero"
All chapters in "Improving Sex"
All chapters in "Perfecting Sleep"
"Reversing 'Permanent' Injuries"

Improving Speed and Endurance
All chapters in "Fundamentals"
All chapters in "Ground Zero"
All chapters in "Running Faster and Farther"

4. It is critical that you choose only one or two goals for yourself at a time. To truly make a change, you must be able to make small habits which will in turn help you achieve your goal. Rank each chapter of topics based on which ones are most important to you. Write these rankings from most important to least important: Priority (I want to follow this topic now) / Meaningful (I want to know more about this but I can wait to follow) / Interesting (I'm interested in the topic to better myself in the future).

Chapter	Importance	Notes
Ex: Subtracting Fat	Meaningful	It's good to know but not my main priority right now
Subtracting Fat		
Adding Muscle		
Improving Sex		
Perfecting Sleep		
Reversing Injuries		
Running Faster and Farther		
Getting Stronger		
From Swimming to Swinging		
On Longer and Better Life		

5. Now that you're familiar with what The 4-Hour Body has to offer, you must again relate each topic back to your personal goals. Go to the second exercise and compare which of your personal goals are most important to you right now and which chapters within the 4HB will guide you. When comparing chapters and goals, seek out the top two goals you wrote for yourself and align them with the appropriate chapters. In the beginning, it is recommended to pick one appearance goal and one performance goal.

Top Appearance Goal	Corresponding Chapters in 4HB
	• • • •

Top Performance Goal	Corresponding Chapters in 4HB
	• • • •

Chapter 2: FIRST AND FOREMOST

The Minimum Effective Dose: From Microwave to Fat-Loss

The Minimum Effective Dose

Everything humans do is centered around the *minimum effective dose (MED)*. This simple directive creates all things in biology and chemistry. It is *the smallest amount of material needed to produce the wanted product*. The MED can be applied to numerous subjects, including strength training. Arthur Jones emphasized that there is a "minimum effective load" needed to achieve a desired strength gain (pg. 43).

Would it not be a waste of energy to go beyond the MED if you've achieved your goal?

Humans get caught doing just that all the time. We water the grass when it's green, work out for two hours every gym session, and charge our phones even though they're at 100%. Ferriss uses the example of boiling water and tanning as his examples of *exceeding the MED*. Boiling water using a higher temperature than 212 °F would just *drain resources that could be used for something else* (pg. 43). Tanning for longer than the MED of 15 minutes would just make you burn and cause you to waste time recovering.

Do the least to stimulate the hormones and local responses necessary.

Muscle gain and fat loss also have their MEDs. However, the 4HB challenges the popular instructions for these topics. Most cookie-cutter regimens will say to "complete 4 sets of 10 repetitions for every exercise" or "cut out all sugars and fats from your diet." *Just because the goals have changed doesn't mean we need to go above the MED to achieve them.*

Finding a simple dose prescription will keep you from exceeding the MED.

Muscular tissue responses could be achieved with only 80 seconds of tension. In other words, you don't need 4 sets of 10 reps if you've used that muscle for 80 seconds already. Finding the "dose prescription" is a key factor to not surpass the MED (aka wasting your time)(pg. 45). Here are a few of Ferriss's examples of dose prescriptions:

1. 80 seconds of 20lb tension
2. 10:00 minutes of 54 °F water
3. 200mg of allicin extract before bed

Rules That Change the Rules: Everything Popular is Wrong

Mentality is the key to the ignition that makes the car run.

Gaining muscle while losing fat is most people's ideal outcome. Ferriss proves you can do it, showing real numbers of gaining muscle and losing fat within a single month. On top of it all, he only worked out for a total of four hours in those 28 days (pg.46). The results sound almost absurd when you compare them to the mainstream fitness/ health advice guides. Perhaps what the fitness gurus are missing isn't just physical changes. How can someone start running if they don't mentally accept that action? You must acquire a happy medium between skepticism and acceptance to make the change.

New Rules for Rapid Redesign

The 4HB lists a few mental models to keep in mind about health and fitness. These models are an accumulation of multiple disciplines to help anyone reading this book elevate themselves.

1. No Exercise Burns Many Calories

Calories are an easy denominator that scientists, publicists, and average citizens can all understand together. **This DOES NOT mean that calories should be your main focus** when trying to build your physique. The 4HB's two central factors will be about:

      a. Heat
      b. Hormones

2. A Drug is a Drug is a Drug

The author emphasizes to not become lost in the science of pharmacology. Trying to distinguish drugs, supplements, or even creams can become confusing. In reality, anything you put into your body that has an effect is a type of drug (pg. 50). It is simpler to **address all remedies under the title of "drug."**

3. The 20-Pound Recomp Goal

The definition of "reduction" is different from "recomposition." When you think of improving your figure, you most likely first think "lose weight." Reducing mass is an important aspect of looking good, but just losing

weight won't make your friends turn around and say "Wow!" Toning and adding muscle, for both females and males, will bring that extra level of physique.
Recomposition is exactly that: **subtracting the unwanted and adding the desired features** (pg.50). Examples of a 20-pound recomposition could look like:

a. Lose: 10 pounds of fat / Gain: 10 pounds of muscle
b. Lose: 15 pounds of fat / Gain: 5 pounds of muscle

4. The 100-Unit Slider: Diet, Drugs, and Exercise

The three components we can adjust are the foods we eat, the drugs we utilize, and the exercise we implement. All three equally divided would be 33% each, adding up to 100% of our desired goal. Ferriss uses a unit slider as a visual tool to describe these split variances:

_____/____/____ (33% diet, 33% drugs, 33% exercise)

It's impossible to keep this perfect split and it's not even the most effective way when talking about fat-loss specifically. Some people will find themselves leaning more toward one component. This could still achieve the goal but would have unhealthy consequences because it's not good for the body. Examples of extreme splits:

/_____/ (100% drugs) = long term side effects
//_____/ (100% exercise) = easily hindered

The ideal fat-loss split would look like this:

_____/_/___ (60% diet, 10% drugs, 30% exercise)

There will be **adjustments based on personal preferences, compliance with the regimen, and worldly interferences** (pg. 52):

_/____/_____ (10% diet, 45% drugs, 45% exercise) = vegan or always traveling

5. *The Duct Tape Test: Will It Stick?*

It is common for people to not stay consistent with their new ambitions. You make a New Year's resolution, buy a gym membership on January 1st, but by mid-February you've found an excuse to not go anymore. Everyone's been there and done that; it's natural. However, you need to find a method, or "slider split," that you can be realistic about achieving. If you need to use another method that is less effective and less efficient, then use it (pg. 52). **Being consistent with an average method, rather than continuously failing perfect methods, is superior.**

6. *Don't Confuse Physical Recreation with Exercise*

Having hobbies is important; they're fun activities that we can look forward to. **Recreational activities are hobbies** and provide an extra element of physical exertion with little to no stress. On the other hand, exercise is a trackable activity with specific movements for a specific goal. You cannot call both the same thing. If you want to have fun, then go out and rock climb for hours. **If you want to make a change, then go exercise.**

7. *Don't Confuse Correlation with Cause and Effect*

A lot of studies can't control every factor that plays a part in the results. Training like a football player won't make you look like one. Why? Because sometimes the guys who are born bigger and broader naturally play football. Three statements to keep in mind about cause and effect:

1. **The arrow of causality is reversed:** Natural-born football players will play football.
2. **Don't mix up absence and presence:** Is drinking more sports drinks replenishing because of their contents or is it just that you're drinking more fluids because sports drinks taste better than plain water?
3. **Testing specific demographics brings other variables to the table:** If you claim a HIIT class will improve cardiorespiratory health, but only tested in the upper-class neighborhood, then money probably contributed to that demographic's great health as well.

In other words, it is important to **stay skeptical of statements that claim A causes B** (pg. 55).

8. *Use the Yo-Yo: Embrace Cycling*

Another natural aspect of human life is cycling diets. It is incredibly difficult to continuously cut or overeat calories every single day. To sustain that type of diet could become more harmful than helpful. On the other hand, scheduling these cuts or gains could be just as effective. Don't tire yourself out by trying to maintain top physical condition all year. Even elite athletes take vacations, and they embrace that time off! **Eat what you want, just time it right** to hit that planned acceleration in your body redesign (pg. 55).

9. *Predisposition vs. Predestination: Don't Blame Your Genes*

You're given certain genetics at birth; it's literally what makes you *you*. However, blaming these genes for not being able to achieve something is absurd. This is because genetics can be modified, redirected, or changed! Some individuals are more predisposed to certain things, like pathologies, negative physical traits, etc. These are important to be aware of but not important enough to be made into an excuse. **Don't let predisposition determine what you are predestined for** (pg56). You are in charge of what you can achieve not your genes.

10. Eliminate Propaganda and Nebulous Terms

"Marketer-speak" and "ambiguous" words are carefully thought-out marketing statements to make the consumer think a certain way (pg. 57). The fitness industry is just that: an industry with business being the top priority. They will use marketing terms to lure customers into believing certain things and ultimately purchasing their products. Examples of "marketer-speak" terms that should be seen as irrelevant are:

1. Toning
2. Cellulite
3. Firming
4. Shaping
5. Aerobics

Examples of "scientific sounding" terms that are overused are:

1. Health
2. Fitness
3. Optimal

All these words cannot be measured and are therefore worthless. When attempting to redesign your body, **you**

need to have measurable quantitative objectives.
Qualitative goals like "I want to have a healthy heart" or
"being fit is my goal" are useless. Making definite goals
like setting a dream mile pace time or increasing your
healthy cholesterol to a certain level are realistic and
definable (pg. 58).

Why a Calorie Isn't a Calorie

Debunking the importance of calories is critical moving
forward. The media has exaggerated the significance of
calories in health. Of course, they're a factor, but they are
far from being the priority. There are two rules Ferriss has
made regarding calories:

1. **It's not the foods you eat that matter, but what
   makes it into your bloodstream.**

Human digestion is just that – digestion. Foods pass
through the body every day and not all of that is released
into the bloodstream. If you eat a piece of cake, not all of it
will be utilized by the body. Therefore, saying that a slice
of cake has around 200 calories is technically inaccurate,
especially adding that the calorie was found from
incinerating foods on fireplace logs, not through the human
stomach (pg. 59).

2. **The body responds differently to carbohydrates
   (CHO), proteins, and fats.**

Every food is made up of different chemical structures.
Some of these structures are harder to break down while
others are easier. The three main components of food
structures are carbohydrates, proteins, and fats. Each is
digested differently and produces varying results:

1,000 cals. At 90% **fat = weight *loss* of 0.9 lbs.** Per day
1,000 cals. At 90% **protein = weight *loss* of 0.6 lbs.** Per day
1,000 cals. At 90% **carbohydrate = weight *gain* of 0.24 lbs.** Per day

To maximize the success rate of a fitness program, three factors can **be modified**:

1. Digestion management
2. The ratio of carbohydrates : proteins : fats
3. Timing of food

Marketing 101: Sexism Sells

The health industry has identified certain populations and exploited them for financial gain. One of those groups is females. This marketing throws out inaccurate health information specifically for women to follow. In reality, both men and women want to lose weight and gain muscle. Having the **same training for identical results** would make sense in that case (pg.62). There is no need to separate and confuse people because of the "gender norms" that capitalism created.

It is important to keep in mind though that biologically women have one-tenth the amount of testosterone that a man does (pg. 62), so achieving massive muscular growth in a short period of time is impossible for a woman. **Being afraid to become "too bulky" without warning is biologically impossible.**

Some scientists propose that women have "more slow-twitch muscle" than men and should therefore "train differently" (pg. 63). As Ferriss said, **train for the goal you want**:

1. Muscle fibers can be changed when trained properly.

2. Eating and incorporating specific training for your specific goal is key.

3. Train and eat as your future self; don't accommodate where you are currently.

Key Points

- Knowing the "minimum effective dose" (MED) will help keep you from doing more than you need to.
- Your body is made up of heavy muscle; keep this in mind during your training if your strength and weight increases simultaneously.
- Be consistent with a method you will stick to rather than a complicated one you'll quit after a month.
- Your body has its own cycle and schedule. Time eating right, and you can still eat what you want.
- Train and eat for who you want to be in the future; don't slack because of the level you're at in the present.

Back To You

1. "Minimum effective dose" is a key term focused on in this chapter. State a habit or a time when you might have exceeded the "MED" and explain what happened because you exceeded the effective dose. Ex: Boiled water for too long and ended up evaporating all the water in the pot.

2. The word "drug" is used as an umbrella term in the 4HB for any supplements, other than food, that you put into your body. List 3 "drugs" you use regularly (daily or weekly). Do some research to see the common effects of those drugs on the human body. Ex: Vitamin C daily – it helps defend against free radicals that could harm the body.

   a.

   b.

   c.

3. The author creates the visual aide "100-unit slider" to divide the three components of diet, drugs, and exercise. Create your own 100-unit slider based on what your preferences are. Add in three slashes to divide each section and title the components with a rough percentage for each. Adjust each component to try to be as realistic as possible to your habits. Ex. If you already enjoy exercising weekly, then put the slider further with "exercise".

_____

4. Predispositions are qualities we have been naturally gifted from our genes. However, people often see these genetics as an excuse for dealing or not dealing with their health. List three genetic traits you might see as negative and provide a positive response for each. Ex: I've never had natural endurance, BUT I can create a progressive running program to take me step by step to running longer distances.

    1.

    2.

    3.

5. Nutrition consists of three main structures: carbohydrates, proteins, and fats. Research three nutritional foods that are mainly composed of one of those structures. Pick foods you enjoy eating or would be willing to try. Ex: Oatmeal is around 70% carbs / Avocadoes are 80% fat.

i. **Carbohydrates**

       1.

       2.

       3.

ii. **Protein**

       1.

       2.

       3.

iii. **Fats**

       1.

       2.

       3.

Chapter 3: Ground Zero: Getting Started and Swaraj

The Harajuku Moment

The Decision to Become a Complete Human

Most people don't stick with their goals because they've never had a deep connection to them. There are **two reasons why people fail**:

1. **Their reason isn't important enough.** If the goal is not seen as a "must-have," then excuses will start piling up (pg.67).
2. **No awareness of progress.** You feel motivated when you see yourself succeed even a little. Consistently tracking your progress can show you the little achievements and keep you focused. If you don't track your progress, then you won't be aware of how well you're progressing. This will allow doubts and excuses to take over because self-manipulation is easy without proof.

The Harajuku Moment

An internal epiphany is the most influential driving force.

Ferriss calls this the "Harajuku Moment" (pg.67). Health is the most important thing in our lives and should be our priority. Being in good health not only keeps us living longer and more functionally, but mentally you will feel better too. However, *being "healthy" has one of the*

***highest failure rates because it's hard to be self-driven
every day*** without a personal "Harajuku Moment." Fitness
can seem like Mt. Everest to you, but little changes and
small steps will eventually get you to the top.

Learning some "fake science" could save you from becoming overwhelmed.

Once you've taken that first step, learning is key. Ferriss
has mentioned that calories are not as fundamental as we
think they are. If you're aware of that fact but can still use
calories as pseudo-science, then you have your data. The
average person doesn't have accurate tools to measure how
much they're burning every day, but ***a rough estimate can
be used to stay on track.***

Oversimplifying calories is easy. Specifically for weight
loss, knowing a rough average of your weight's basal
metabolic rate (aka resting metabolic rate) can help. It
shows you the amount of energy (calories) needed just to
keep your body functioning at rest. An example of
simplifying these numbers for a deficit estimate can be
shown as this:

BMR = 2,900 calories

Actual intake = 1,800 calories
Deficit from diet = BMR - actual intake = 2,900 - 1,800 =
1,100 calories

Burned from 30 minutes of cardio = 500 calories

Total deficit = deficit from diet + burned from 30 minutes
of cardio = 1,600 calories lost in one day

The key to this kind of thought process is remembering that *these numbers should only be directionally right, not 100% accurate.* Meal planning can be one of those "directionally right" steps. Having an exact meal plan for one week at a time is easy, and that's the name of the game. So, create that meal plan for the week with another rough estimate as to how many calories you're eating with each meal. It takes one trip to the grocery store to buy the ingredients to have your entire week's meals set.

Finding your heart rate zones and the corresponding calories burned is simple data.

Another daily tool to look into is a heart rate monitor (HRM). These are super accessible to anyone and can give you another set of data to be aware of. Most digital watches these days have HRMs incorporated in them and sometimes even other tools for health data. You'll be able to associate everyday tasks with your current HR zone, not just exercise.

Elusive Body Fat

Where Are You Really?

The Deceptive Scale

Body composition is not just how much you weigh on a scale.

You have to remember that you will lose weight, but you will also plateau or even gain weight as well. This plateau or gain will happen because you are adding lean muscle to your body composition. Muscle is deceptively heavy but in the best way possible. *Embrace your strength gains.*

Choosing the Right Tools

Using a scale for weight gives only a general idea of what your body composition looks like. Along with the other "directional" data, *scales should be used periodically and not be solely relied on* as the main source of progress. Using circumference with a measuring tape can get you closer to truly seeing what your current body fat percentage is.

Skinning the Cat

There are numerous ways to test body fat percentage and Ferriss has personally tried all of them:

- Circumference
- BioElectrical Impedance
- Skinfold
- Ultrasound
- BodPod
- Underwater Weighing
- DEXA
- X-ray CT
- MRI

He provides the three best options based on expense, accuracy, and convenience.

The Top 3

1. **Dual-energy X-ray absorptiometry (DEXA)**
   a. $50-100 per session
   b. Error % = ~1.2% - 2.0%

        c. Measures:
            i. Body fat percentage
            ii. Lean mass
            iii. Bone density
            iv. Muscle imbalance
2. **BodPod**
    a. $25-50 per session
    b. Error % = ~2.3% - 2.8%
    c. Measures:
        i. Body fat percentage
3. **BodyMetrix (Ultrasound)**
    a. Dependent on the medical provider (low)
    b. Error % = ~2.3% - 3.0%
    c. Measures:
        i. Body fat percentage
        ii. Muscular thickness

Can't Find the Fancy Stuff?

Most people can't afford to get regularly measured by the three provided options. Instead, there are *cheaper, more convenient tools like calipers or bio-impedance devices*. The author states three important points to keep in mind when using these tools:

1. Don't compare results from different tools.

Because of differing error possibilities, no two tools can be compared. If you did, you could come to the false conclusion that you lost or gained 2% body fat depending on the order you used each instrument.

2. Bioelectrical impedance (BEI) devices require consistent hydration levels.

These gadgets function by sending safe electrical currents through your body's tissues. Each type of tissue allows the current to pass through at various speeds. Muscle and water travel fast, while body fat slows the current.

The 4HB recommends these steps to ensure accurate and reliable BEI measurements:

- Drink 1.5 liters of cold water as soon as you wake up
- Don't eat or drink anything else before testing
- Test at the same time of day, after the same steps have been completed
- Wait 30 minutes after hydrating to test

3. Use the same algorithm when using calipers

Caliper results will vary depending on the user taking the measurements and the math used for the final percentage. To ensure reliability follow these steps:

- Have the same physician measure you each time
- Use the same anatomical points each time on the same side
- Use the 3-point or 7-point Jackson-Pollock algorithm

Starting Your Physical GPS – The Steps

Use measurements during your body recomposition journey.

9 times out of 10 you research something before you do it. You wouldn't go for a hike on a new trail without a map. Using measurements can keep you on track physically and mentally. Here are some steps to start taking:

1. Take "before" measurements of circumference with a tape measure. Add up the measurements found to get your Total Inches (TI). Measure these four areas:

    1. Both arms at mid-bicep
    2. Waist (horizontal to your belly button)
    3. Hips (point that is widest below waist)
    4. Both legs at mid-thigh

2. Estimate your body fat percentage by comparing yourself to the "Eyeballing It" pictures on page 92.
3. Compare the various measuring examples and pick/schedule an appointment for one of them.
    a. Over 30% BF
        i. Avoid calipers
        ii. Use DEXA, BodPod, or ultrasound (IN THAT ORDER)
        iii. If these are not available, use BEI with the hydration rules
    b. Under 25% BF
        i. Use DEXA, BodPod, or ultrasound
        ii. If these are not available use calipers with a qualified professional

1. Use the suggestions stated above under "calipers"
iii. If that is not available, use a different algorithm and write down the name and math included with it

From Photos to Fear

Making Failure Impossible

Mentality is a driving force for people to make change. What truly drives someone varies greatly from person to person, and finding that reason within yourself can be challenging. ***Even though people say they're self-driven, they're probably not.*** Instead, think of external factors that could provide that extra push to get you going, like making small bets with your close friends.

Cheap Insurance – Failure Proofing with Four Principles

It is possible to make a foolproof plan for yourself that you won't deviate from. Being self-driven is nearly impossible, which is normal. Here are four principles to make a fool-proof plan:

1. **Make It Conscious**: Flashing and "Before" Photos

> **To correct a behavior, you must first be conscious of it in the moment.**

It is critical to be aware of your choices before you take action. Studies have shown that ***taking "before" pictures will curb that devil on your shoulder before you act***. Food-wise, ***take pictures of the food you eat before you eat it.***

An even better option would be to send it to someone else or post it somewhere others can see. Having that external factor of analyzing your own nutritional choices AND being analyzed by someone else could help put the food you eat regularly into a bigger perspective.

Physique-wise, *take pictures before you start your journey, and – better yet – print that photo* and put it in a place you'll see often. *Don't ignore where your starting point is.* It's just that: the beginning. It's not the end, so embrace it and use it as motivation.

2. **Make It a Game**: Jack Stack and the Stickiness of Five Sessions

   A feedback loop that is positive is when a positive increase results in more production of that reaction.

   An example of this is going to the gym and feeling confident and productive after your workout. This positive reaction will make you increase workouts per week so you can feel good more frequently.

   Some companies have accentuated this feedback loop by creating rewards and public recognition when workers show progress (pg. 112). "The Hawthorne Effect" aka "observer effect" also increases productivity because workers feel their work is being watched by their superiors. Both phenomena support the simple equation that *"measurement = motivation"* (pg.112).

   These can act as a replacement for self-motivation. To get to that point of replacement, consistency is needed. A magical number of 5 has been researched by Nike+ to go from trying it out to becoming hooked (pg.114). *If we can stay consistent with our small steps, then we will see it as more of a game rather than an effort.* "Take five" is what Ferriss has dubbed it. Working out five times, eating five planned meals, or doing five of what we want every week is the goal.

3. **Make It Competitive**: Fear of Loss and the Benefits of Comparison

   The fear of losing something is more powerful than gaining a reward.

   Knowing that losing will motivate you allows you to use public failure to your advantage. We've always been told to ignore peer pressure, but why not embrace it? Being a part of a group has proven to have greater results because of the added emotions of guilt and public humiliation. Create a group of individuals you can healthily compare yourself to and trust to push you in the right direction.

4. **Make it Small and Temporary**

   Ferriss provides four actions for you to pick from to stay consistent right from the start (pg. 115). These four actions are small but meaningful. You need to *pick at least two* and start your journey with these habits.

   1.Do I really look like that in underwear?

   Take that "before" picture while in either undergarments or a bathing suit. Take a photo from the front, side, and back. Then, print and place those pictures in your house somewhere obvious (ex. bathroom mirror, refrigerator, etc.).

2. Do I really eat that?

Take a photo of everything you eat for 3-5 days. Use the size of your hand next to the food as a reference. Put these photos online where others can see (ex. Eat.ly, BodySpace, etc.).

3. Who can I get to do this with me?

Use peer pressure to your advantage and find one person you can compete with against using total inches (TI) or body fat percentage. This competitive edge will be your external drive for progress.

4. How do I measure up?

Find the circumference of these five locations!
- i. Both arms (mid-bicep)
- ii. Waist (horizontal to belly button)
- iii. Hips (widest point under waist)
- iv. Both legs (mid-thigh)

Key Points

- You have two options when it comes to making a change: either you push yourself or you find external help to motivate you.
- Measure your progress from the very beginning to the end. Stay consistent. Use numbers to motivate you but be wary of how accurate they may be.
- Find people to compete with. Peer pressure can be good.

- DEXA, BodPod, and ultrasound machines are the gold standard for measuring body fat percentage.
- Use the four principles of "Failure-Proofing" to keep you motivated even on the hard days.

Back To You

1. Just 30 minutes of cardio can burn approximately 300-500 calories. Find three different examples of low-intensity cardio that suit you.

    i.

    ii.

    iii.

2. Measure your circumferences. Find or buy a tape measure TODAY. Once acquired, write down the measurements you find (in inches). Add the findings together for your sum "Total Inches."

    i. Both arms at mid-bicep

        1. _____ inches

        2. _____ inches

   ii. Waist (horizontal to your belly button)

       1. _____ inches

   iii. Hips (widest point below waist)

       1. _____ inches

   iv. Both legs at mid-thigh

       1. _____ inches

       2. _____ inches

   v. TOTAL INCHES (TI): _____ inches

3. Schedule an appointment. Even if you can't consistently afford one of the "Top 3" option, scheduling an appointment with a professional to get your first measurements will get you started. Compare and contrast between the "Top 3" to determine which is most accessible to you. List the pros and cons of each method below.

	DEXA	BodPod	Ultrasound
Location (address)			

Distance (miles)			
Facility Phone Number			
Cost per Session			
Earliest Availability			

4. Competition was a key topic in this chapter. When used correctly, a game between people can produce high-quality results. Think about people in your life that you could challenge with this journey. Also, research fitness platforms where you can post things, such as food or measurement updates, to compete against/with others. Find at least three of either option and list them below.

i.

ii.

iii.

5. Ferriss emphasizes starting right now with simple
   steps. He gives four actions to choose from and put
   into action immediately. Because you already
   completed your measurements, what are the three
   remaining "small and temporary" actions you can
   take?

i.

ii.

iii.

Chapter 4: Subtracting Fat: Basics

The Slow Carb Diet I

How to Lose 20 Pounds in 30 Days Without Exercise

The Slow-Carb Diet: Better Fat-Loss Through Simplicity

Ferriss introduces a diet that will provide fat-loss results. By emphasizing the nutrition component of the "100-unit slider," remember to still incorporate some exercise or supplements. There are *five rules for the Slow-Carb Diet:*

1. Avoid "White" Carbohydrates

White or "enriched" carbohydrates contain chlorine dioxide to make the carb white. This chemical combines with protein to form alloxan. Alloxan can cause diabetes, so avoiding this in turn avoids gaining fat. *Avoid these foods:*

1. Bread
2. Rice (white or brown)
3. Cereal
4. Potatoes
5. Pasta
6. Tortillas
7. Fried food with breading
8. Anything white

These foods are only allowed to be ingested within 30 minutes of finishing a resistance-training workout (pg. 130). Go to "From Geek to Freak" or "Occam's Protocol" for examples of those workouts.

2. Eat the Same Few Meals Over and Over Again

Eating the same meals over and over can produce muscle gain or fat loss. The author provides a list of foods to mix and match to make meals you would find enjoyable. The foods with stars have shown fast results of fat loss for Ferriss specifically.

1. Proteins
    a. *Egg whites
        i. With 1-2 whole eggs (for flavor)
        ii. 2-5 whole eggs including yolks (if organic)
    b. *Chicken breast or thigh
    c. *Beef (grass-fed)
    d. *Fish
    e. *Pork

2. Legumes
    a. *Lentils
    b. *Black beans
    c. Pinto beans
    d. Red beans
    e. Soybeans

3. Vegetables
    a. *Spinach
    b. *Mixed vegetables
        i. Include broccoli, cauliflower, or any cruciferous vegetable
    c. *Sauerkraut, kimchi
    d. Asparagus

e. Peas

f. Broccoli

g. Green beans

The options you can pick from are given above, keep it simple and plan 3-4 meals. Even *when dining out, substitute French fries for a salad or a side of vegetables.* It is a small switch that will make a big difference to your meal.

A low-carb diet can result in an insufficient amount of calories.

Your low-carb meals must provide enough calories for you, or you'll find yourself with low energy. *Legumes can add an adequate number of calories.* If needed, you can supplement with extra meals per day, but if your meals are built correctly, you should be just fine. The timing of meals is also important. *Keep in mind that each meal should be around four hours apart.*

Ferriss provides a few of his meal examples:

Breakfast (Home)
I. Scrambled Eggology (pourable egg whites) + 1 whole egg
II. Black beans
III. Mixed vegetables

Lunch (Mexican restaurant)
I. Grass-fed organic beef
II. Pinto beans
III. Mixed vegetables
IV. Extra guacamole

Dinner (Home)
I. Grass-fed organic beef
II. Lentils
III. Mixed vegetables

3. Don't Drink Calories

Drinks to prioritize:
1. Water
2. Unsweetened tea
3. Coffee (no more than two Tbsp. of cream)
4. No-calorie or low-calorie beverages
5. Limit red wine to two per day

Drinks to exclude:
1. Milk (even soy milk)
2. Soft drinks
3. Fruit juice
4. Limit diet soft drinks to 16 oz. per day
5. White wines or beer

4.Don't Eat Fruit

Fruit contains useful vitamins and minerals, but it is not necessary to eat them every day. The sugar and fructose in fruit is converted to GP (glycerol phosphate) quickly, even faster than carbohydrates. Glycerol phosphate is converted to triglycerides and stored as fat.

Fructose → glycerol phosphate → triglycerides → fat storage

5. Take One Day Off Per Week

Don't count calories and eat whatever your heart desires for one day.

Being this strict without a cheat day isn't enjoyable at all. *Allow yourself one day out of the week to "treat yourself."* You shouldn't try to tough it out and eat by your diet on this day either.

Spiking your caloric intake once per week will increase fat loss because your metabolic rate is kept at a high rate. If you were to follow the diet 24/7, your body would detect this and adapt to a slower metabolic rate. *Spiking the calories dramatically will keep your metabolism on its toes and burn fat fast.*

Try to make the cheat day at the end of your week. By following the diet for five consecutive days and "cheating" on Saturday, it'll be easier to get back on track after the binge.

$1.34 Per Meal?

Meal planning can be tedious for multiple reasons. A lot of people find that expenses are a setback for buying nutritional food. Ferriss wanted to provide some examples of meals and the cost for each item to give some ideas:

Breakfast
       I. Egg whites
       II. One whole egg
       III. Mixed vegetables
       IV. Chicken breast

Lunch

I. Mixed vegetables

II. Peas

III. Spinach (salad)

Second Lunch

I. Chicken thigh

II. Black beans

III. Mixed vegetables

Dinner

I. Beef (or pork)

II. Asparagus

III. Pinto beans

COST

1x eggs (12 pack) $1.20
2x Grass-fed organic beef (0.5-lb cuts) $4
4x Mixed vegetables (1-lb bags) $6
2x Pork (1-lb cuts) $3
1x Chicken breast $2
2x Asparagus bundles $2
1x Organic peas (2-lb bag) $2
1x Pinto beans (1-lb bag) $1.50
2x Spinach (3-lb bags) $6
1x Black beans (1-lb bag) $1
3x Chicken thigh $9

Total per week: $37.70

The Forbidden Fruit: Fructose

Fructose is a type of sugar found within fruits. This sugar is also found in multiple fruit juices. Ferriss used orange juice as the independent variable in his diet. The changes shown are from two weeks of no fructose compared to two weeks of drinking orange juice (fructose):

Cholesterol: 203 → 243 (out of "healthy" range)

LDL: 127 → 165 (out of "healthy" range)

Albumin: 4.3 → 4.9 (noticeable jump)

Iron: 71 → 191 (extremely out of "healthy" range)

Iron had the unhealthiest jump. An increase in iron is not ideal for men because their bodies don't clear extra iron as well as females. Excessive iron in men could become toxic.

The Slow Carb Diet II

The Finer Points and Common Questions

Diets can be intimidating; that's why there's a high failure rate. The 4HB wants to eliminate those fears and provide realistic solutions to common problems.

Common Questions and Concerns

1. How can I follow this diet? It's too strict!

Change one meal a day to the diet. For example, start with altering your breakfast only for six days of the week. You will see results from even one adjusted meal a day. Plus, you can still indulge on your cheat day.

Tips:

- *Write down what you're craving* in the moment. You can eat this on your cheat day.

- *Sugar-free Jell-O* is a good option to satisfy a sweet craving.

2. But eating the same stuff is so boring!

Although this diet calls for specific foods, chances are you eat the same meals throughout the week normally. The difference between your meals and this diet is that *you will see results, so the monotony is worth it!* It is guaranteed you'll look and feel better by rotating the meals for a few weeks.

Tips:

- *Add different seasonings* or light sauces to mix up the taste
- *The cheat day is there for a reason...* enjoy it!
- Meal examples:
  - Breakfast
    - Egg whites
    - Lentils
    - Broccoli
  - Lunch
    - Burrito bowl
      - Chicken
      - Black beans
      - Veggies
  - Dinner
    - Chicken
      - Lentils
      - Assorted veggies

3. Should I take any supplements?

Yes! The slow-carb diet will have you lose excess water so electrolytes will help replenish your body. The three supplements to look into are:

I. Potassium
    A. Potassium-enriched salt ("Lite Salt")
    B. Avocados (extra guacamole)
    C. 99-milligram tablets with each meal

II. Magnesium
    A. 500 mg before bed can help sleep

III. Calcium
    A. Easiest in pill form

Whole food examples:
Potassium
- *Lima beans* / cooked / 4.9 cups (1 cup = 969 mg)
- *Chard* / cooked / 4.9 cups (1 cup= 961 mg)
- *Halibut* / cooked / 2.6 filets (½ filet = 916 mg)
- *Spinach* / cooked / 5.6 cups (1 cup= 839 mg)
- *Pinto beans* / cooked / 6.3 cups (1 cup= 746 mg)
- *Lentils* / cooked / 6.4 cups (1 cup= 731 mg)
- *Salmon* / cooked / 3.4 filets (½ filet = 683 mg)
- *Black beans* / cooked / 7.7 cups (1 cup = 611 mg)
- *Sardines* / 7.9 cups (1 cup = 592 mg)
- *Mushrooms* / cooked / 8.5 cups (1 cup = 555 mg)

Magnesium
- *Pumpkin seeds (pepitas)* / 2.6 oz (2 oz = 300 mg)
- *Watermelon seeds* / dried / 2.8 oz (2 oz = 288 mg)
- *Peanuts* / 1.6 cups (1 cup = 245 mg)

- *Halibut* / cooked / 1.2 filets (½ filet = 170 mg)
- *Almonds* / 5 oz (2 oz = 160 mg)
- *Spinach* / 2.5 cups (1 cup = 157 mg)
- *Soybeans* / cooked / 2.7 cups (1 cup = 148 mg)
- *Cashews* / 5.5 oz (2 oz = 146 mg)
- *Pine nuts* / 5.7 oz (2 oz = 140 mg)
- *Brazil nuts* / 6.3 tbsp (2 tbsp = 128 mg)

Calcium
- *Salmon with bones* / 1.1 cups (1 cup = 919 mg)
- *Sardines with bones* / 1.8 cups (1 cup = 569 mg)
- *Mackerel* / canned / 2.2 cups (1 cup = 458 mg)
- *Tofu/firm* / 3.6 cups (1 cup = 280 mg)
- *Collards* / cooked / 3.8 cups (1 cup = 266 mg)
- *Spinach* / cooked / 4.1 cups (1 cup = 245 mg)
- *Black-eyes peas* / cooked / 4.7 cups (1 cup = 211 mg)
- *Turnip greens* / cooked / 5.1 cups (1 cup = 107 mg)
- *Tempeh* / 5.4 cups (1 cup = 184 mg)
- *Agar* / dried / 5.7 cups (1 oz. = 175 mg)

4. **No dairy? Really? Doesn't milk have a low glycemic index?**

Dairy does have a low glycemic index of 27. This means dairy has a slow impact on blood sugar levels, which is good. However, it does have a high insulinemic index of 90-98. This means that *dairy increases insulin levels the same as white bread.*

Tips:

- *Removing any dairy will accelerate fat loss.*

- *For coffee,* use no more than 2 tbsp of cream, *try dashes of cinnamon or vanilla extract instead*

5. No fruit? Don't I need a "balanced diet?"

A balanced diet has not been officially defined by the U.S. Department of Agriculture. *Needing to eat as much fruit as society states you do is false advertisement.* For fat loss, remove excess fruit.

Tips:

- See "The Forbidden Fruit" section for more information about fruit.

6. God, I hate beans. Can I substitute something else?

It's normal to not enjoy beans for a variety of reasons. Ferriss goes into those possible reasons and advises adjusting to this diet.

Upset stomach from beans:
- *Lentils*
- *Purchase organic beans*
- *Soak beans in water for a few hours*
    - Breaks down oligosaccharides
- *Canned beans*
    - Drain can juice
    - Rinse beans
        - *Add Beano or Bean-zyme* (vegan option) *or epazote* (Mexican grocery stores)

The bland taste of beans:
- *Add balsamic vinegar and garlic powder*

- *Hot sauce*
- *Red beans instead of black or pinto*

Bean feel and texture:
- *Fake mashed potatoes*
  - White kidney beans, cauliflower, or refried beans
  - Mash in a pan with:
    - Olive oil
    - Water
    - Seasoning
    - Cheese

Do I have to eat beans for every meal??
- *No, order extra vegetables and protein instead*
- *Slow-carb appetizers*
  - Unbreaded calamari
  - Salad with vinegar and olive oil
- *Eat, eat, eat*
  - You still need to get enough calories in your meals

7. **I gained 8 pounds after my cheat day! Did I mess up my progress?**

It is normal to gain weight after a cheat day. You are having an increase in water weight because of the carbohydrate intake. Women can gain up to 8 pounds easily after a cheat day, while men can gain 10-20 pounds.

The important thing is to not just focus on the weight fluctuations but also on the inches. *You will lose inches and it is crucial to regularly measure your circumferences.* Muscle weighs more than fat, and you will gain lean muscle. The weight can be deceptive, but the measurements won't be.

8. Can I use salt, spices, or light sauces? What can I cook with?

Tips:

- *Yes:* spices and herbs > *No:* cream-based sauces
- *Ingredients to use:*
    - Montreal steak rub
    - Thick salsa (without sugar)
    - Garlic salt
    - White truffle sea salt
        - Combine with tarragon on eggs
    - Thai chili paste (sriracha)
- *Salad dressing alternatives:*
    - Non-sugar sweeteners
        - Stevia mixed with vinegar and mustard
    - Balsamic vinegar and olive oil
- *Butter is ok*
    - If it is purely made out of butter and salt

The New and Improved Olive Oil? Introducing Macadamia Oil

The pros of macadamia oil:

I. *Tastes like butter*
II. *Higher smoking point than olive oil*
    A. Can be used for sauteing

III. Long shelf life
    A. Doesn't become spoiled from light exposure like olive oil

IV. Has a high level of palmitoleic acid
    A. Only plant oil offers this
    B. This is a healthy fatty acid

V. 80% monounsaturated fat
    A. A healthy type of fat
    B. The body can break it down easier than other types of fats

9. Can I drink alcohol? What types of wine are the best?

Yes, you can drink alcohol. On cheat days drink whatever you want. However, during the diet week *stick to dry wines* (less than 1.4% residual sugar).

    Dry red wines:
- Pinot Noir
- Cabernet Sauvignon
- Merlot

    Dry white wines:
- Sauvignon Blanc
- Albariño

Ferriss has found ***better fat loss results from drinking red wine compared to white wine.*** He states he still indulges in some bigger red wines such as Malbec and Zinfandel. Based on his research, Ferriss advises to ***avoid Riesling, White Zinfandel, and Champagne.***

10. What should I eat for snacks?

Snacks can be a product of not eating enough calories or a psychological addiction.

If you find yourself hungry:

- *Add more protein or legumes to your meals*
- *Eat another slow-carb meal*
- *Eat a bag of carrots*
- *With this diet, eat meals that are 2-3 times bigger*

You might experience trouble sleeping because of hunger. If this occurs, ***try eating some protein before bed.*** A tablespoon of almond butter or peanut butter (no additives) can help fill your stomach.

11. Do I really have to binge once a week?

Yes, you should. It may sound absurd or even forced, but binging during a diet is a natural response. ***It is better to plan these binges ahead of time rather than lose control.*** Spiking your calories once a week sends hormones on a crazy ride that keeps the body in fat-loss mode. It keeps the body from becoming accustomed to your diet. Your metabolism will stay active because of this random excess of calories and "different" foods.

12. Can you get away with one cheat meal per week?

No, most people, male or female, can't get away with so few cheat moments. Specifically for women, menstruation stays consistent when leptin levels do. ***If you don't indulge*** in cheat days, then these levels will drop and ***you could temporarily pause your menstruation cycle.*** "Forced overfeeding" can increase these leptin levels by 40% (pg. 155).

Cheat days should be done once per week.

Cheat days are not only a good physical trick. Mentally is useful as a reset for the next week of dieting. For those who get nervous about cheat days, try eating a high-protein breakfast and then spend the rest of the day binging (pg. 155).

Be sure to eat all your cheat meal foods before the next day.

If there is leftover food, you will find yourself eating it throughout the week when you shouldn't.

13. What about breakfast?

The classic American breakfast usually consists of a carbohydrate as the main entree. For this diet, you must replace that carb with protein. Eggs, lentils, and spinach can do this for you. This may take out the traditional breakfast feel. However, you can make breakfast smaller, with 30% protein, and eat a bigger lunch in just a few hours.

A more typical breakfast meal:
- Eggs (try cooking with clarified butter (ghee))
- Turkey bacon or organic normal bacon
- Sliced tomato
- Cottage cheese

Geek's Advantage: Eggs, Lentils and Spinach

I. Eggs
A. Proven fat loss
B. Proven increased basal metabolism

Eggs have been researched to decrease weight by 65% and reduce waist circumference in 83% of women. This result was achieved by replacing a breakfast bagel with two eggs each day for only eight weeks.

The egg yolk provides choline. This nutrient provides liver protection and increases fat loss. Choline also breaks down into betaine. It is an amino acid that provides muscle growth and repair.

II. Spinach
A. Increases muscle growth
B. Increases protein synthesis
C. Increases muscular performance

Amount of spinach needed per day to see results:
- *2 cups (162 grams) = 16% of 1 kg*
  - 3% increase in muscle fiber synthesis
- *3 cups = 25% 1 kg*
  - 5% increase in muscle fiber synthesis

III. Lentils
A. High source of protein
B. High source of isoleucine and lysine
   1. Branched-chain amino acids
   2. Muscular repair

3. Decreased plasma glucose levels
4. Increased muscle glucose levels

14. Do I have to limit veggies to those listed?

You are more than welcome to eat any type of vegetable you want. Ferriss has noticed that *the more variety in the diet foods, the more likely people are to quit.* Diets need structure to stay simple and easy to commit to. You can substitute any vegetable you want.

Tips:
- *Eat lentils for caloric density*
- *Cauliflower is underrated!*
  - *Makes great fake mashed potatoes*
  - *Don't eat other white-colored foods*

15. Are canned foods alright?

Canned and frozen foods are perfectly fine!

16. Can I eat whole grains or steel-cut oats?

Ferriss responds to this question with a simple *"No"* (pg. 159).

17. Can I do this if I'm lacto-ovo vegetarian?

Being lacto-ovo doesn't inhibit you from following this diet. *Eggs and beans will be your best friends to replace meat.* Go to "Meatless Machine" for more alternatives.

Tips:

Foods that are ok to eat:
- *Cottage cheese*
  - *High casein levels facilitate fat loss (pg.159)*
- *Veggie hot dogs*
- *Instone high-protein pudding*
- *Brown rice*
- *Hemp or pea protein*

Foods to avoid:
- *Refined soy products*
- *Soy milk*
- *Isolated soy protein supplements*

18. Can I eat salsa?

Salsa is a great addition to the slow-carb diet! It adds extra flavor and calories to the repetitive meals. Chunky medium spicy salsa that has corn, beans, etc. is a perfect option (pg. 160). However, be cautious of combining salsa and lentils because it's not tasty.

19. Can I eat fried foods?

Stir fry is ideal while deep-fry should be avoided entirely. Refried beans are acceptable and have even been used as the main entree in meals. If you have an elevated cholesterol level, be wary of only eating refried beans. They contain 45% of our daily allowance of sodium in just one cup. Mix in different types of beans to decrease water retention.

20. What if I'm traveling and eating in airports?

There are plenty of options to satisfy your hunger when traveling in airports. *Try to find a grill or Mexican restaurant. If you can't, get a bag of walnuts and raw almonds*. Avoid starch for the rest of your travel time. You should also be able to find a simple chicken salad. Be sure to only have olive oil or vinegar for the dressing.

Eating Out and The Chipotle Method

The slow-carb diet can be followed even when you go out to eat. The author states to simply ask for "more vegetables instead of [starches]" (pg. 161). *Switch out the rice, bread, or potato for any kind of vegetable.* Usually, this is an available option for free. Even if it isn't for free, you can pay just a dollar or two more for the switch.

Here is an example of the meals from the slow-carb "Chipotle Diet":

Breakfast:
- One cup of coffee
- Two eggs (scrambled or hard-boiled)

Lunch:
- Fajita bowl
  - Peppers
  - Onions
  - Steak
  - Tomato salsa
  - Green tomatillo salsa
  - Cheese
  - Sour cream
  - Guacamole
  - Romaine lettuce

Dinner:

- Same Fajita bowl as above ^^

    Total calories: 1,480 calories
    29 grams of non-fiber carbohydrates daily

21. What about fat loss drugs?

Although fat loss drugs can be implemented, it isn't worth the risk of addiction or bodily damage. *PAGG is recommended for its effectiveness and safety from side effects.* Go to "The Four Horsemen" for more information.

22. Isn't higher protein hard on the kidneys? What if I have gout?

Do not modify your medication or start a new diet without consultation from a medical professional.

Based on Ferriss' research, there is a lack of evidence to support the claim that protein can hurt the kidneys. *Fructose (sugar) and phosphoric acid in carbonated drinks are more likely to cause gout than protein.* Ferriss' mother followed the slow-carb diet and took her low-dose allopurinol medication throughout. The food was the only change and despite the increase in protein, her uric acid levels dropped to within healthy range.

23. I'm hitting a plateau. What should I do?

There are *three common mistakes* people make that cause a plateau:

1. *Eating too late*
2. *Not eating enough protein*
3. *Drinking too little water*

Incorporating just 20 minutes per week of targeted exercise will help increase the rate of fat loss and prevent a standstill. Refer to "Adding Muscle" for exercise options.

Common Mistakes and Misunderstandings

The following problems are common, and each has easy adjustments that will help prevent stalling. If you hit a plateau with fat loss, see if you fall under any of these categories.

1. **Not eating within one hour of waking (at least within 30 minutes)**

   Do not skip breakfast; it could cause overeating in the afternoon. Even if you have no appetite in the morning, eat something small and packed with protein. *You should be eating within the hour that you wake up.* Two to three hard-boiled eggs with some white truffle sea salt will do the trick (pg. 165).

2. **Not eating enough protein**

   Each meal needs to contain at least twenty grams of protein.

   Breakfast should be mainly protein-based. 40% of the calories from your meal should be protein, aka 20 grams of protein (pg.166). At the beginning of this process, it will feel forced and difficult to stomach. However, you have to remember you need to double or triple your food intake on this diet because of the limited carbs. If you restrict your calories, you will become irritable because you're simply not ingesting enough energy.

Tips:

- *Eat 2-3 whole eggs at breakfast*
  - *Add other protein-rich foods to switch it up*
    - *Turkey bacon*
    - *Organic bacon*
    - *Organic sausage*
    - *Cottage cheese*
  - *30-gram protein shake*
    - *With ice and water*
    - *Not dairy*
- *Protein > vegetables*
  - *Don't prioritize the vegetables*
  - *You won't get enough calories*

3. Not drinking enough water

Hydration is important regardless of what diet you're on.

Liver function must be at peak function to ensure fat loss. Even adding a few more glasses of water a day can prevent plateaus in progress. ***On cheat days, drink some extra water.*** The carbohydrates will pull water from your body to the digestive tract.

4. Believing that you'll cook, especially if you're a bachelor

Focus on food selection first and then food preparation.

Most people don't cook and that's ok. Don't go into this diet believing that you suddenly will become a professional chef. You will fall back into your old habits. ***Get frozen*** *food, canned food, or anything easy to make.* Change one thing at a time.

5. **Mis-timing weighings with your menstrual cycle (not a problem for men)**

   During a woman's menstrual cycle, water fluctuation will change measurements.

Don't focus on scale readings in the 10 days leading up to menstruation (pg. 168). You will retain water, and it will throw your weight off. Pay attention to the first weighing following your period for the "after" measurement. *Be aware of your menstruation cycle because you will lose fat.*

6. **Overeating "domino foods"**

   It is easy to plateau in progress when eating "domino foods."

Everyone has picked up a food, said they'll just have one, and accidently ate the whole bag. Get these "domino foods" out of reach and even out of the house to prevent over-snacking. Even though the snacks listed above are nutritious, if you eat too much in one sitting, you will consume more calories than a whole meal. *Assume you will have no self-discipline during this diet and get rid of those foods.* Follow the program exactly as Ferriss has written out and you will see results.

7. **Overconsuming artificial (or "all-natural") sweeteners, including agave nectar**

Artificial sweeteners and agave nectar still increase insulin release (weight gain). These sweeteners still contain a lot of fructose which has just as bad an effect on the metabolism as straight sugar.

> *Tips:*
> - *Avoid sweeteners*
> - *Use spices*
>   - *Cinnamon*
>   - *Vanilla*

8. Hitting the gym too often

Less exercise is more.

By going to the gym, you could over-reward yourself. Although you might gain strength in the beginning, if you overtrain you will lose it. Over-rewarding yourself will only add to a reverse in progress. This can be seen as sports drinks, overeating, and other "treats" being eaten on non-cheat days.

Tips:
- *No more than 2-3 workouts per week*
  - *Working out is not mandatory*
- *Track body fat %*
  - *Don't just look at the scale*

Damage Control

Preventing Fat Gain When You Binge

The Lost Art of Bingeing

Self-experimentation over numerous years allowed Ferriss to master the art of binge eating. ***When eating, either have it go directly to or out of the body or muscle tissue.*** Following these three principles will keep you from gaining weight:

1. **Minimize insulin release, which is a storage hormone**

   To minimize insulin, you must decrease any sudden spike in blood sugar.

   a. *The first meal should be high in protein and insoluble fiber*
      i. 30 grams of protein
         1. Decrease the desire for more binging
      ii. Legumes will handle the fiber
         1. Prevent diarrhea

   b. *Consume a small amount of fructose before the second meal*
      i. Small fructose doses can decrease blood glucose spikes
      ii. Grapefruit juice is recommended

   c. *Use AGG and PAGG supplements*
      i. Increases insulin sensitivity
         1. The pancreas doesn't send as much insulin despite a glucose spike

   d. *Drink citric juices*
      i. Lime juice in water
      ii. Lemon juice on food

iii. Beverage
    1. Citrus kombucha

2. Increase the speed of gastric emptying, or how quickly food exits the stomach

Another tactic during binge eating is to have the food leave the body as fast as possible. By doing this, you reduce the amount of food being absorbed… you keep the trash out of the bloodstream. ***Ferriss has found that caffeine and yerba mate tea will do the trick.***

Tips:
- *Tea that includes theobromine and theophylline*
- *Consume 100-200 milligrams of caffeine OR 16 ounces of cooled yerba mate*
  - *With binging meals*
- *"Athletic Greens" a greens supplement*
  - *Doesn't contain caffeine*

3. Engage in brief muscular contractions throughout the binge

Doing 60-90 seconds of contraction before and after each meal will ward off glucose storage.

Glucose transporter type 4 (GLUT-4) is brought to the surface of the muscle after muscular contraction. This opens the gate for calories to go through and minimizes the amount of food that would trigger the same response with insulin and GLUT-4 on fat cells. ***Put the calories into the muscle before it adds to the fat.***

280 seconds of high-intensity training (HIT) increases GLUT-4 activity by 83%. In contrast, 6 hours of low-intensity training (LIT) activates 91% of GLUT-4 activity.

Tips:

- *60-120 seconds of exercise right before the meal*
  - Activate GLUT-4 before insulin
- *60-90 seconds of exercise 1.5 hours after meal*
  - When blood glucose is at its highest after eating
- *30-50 repetitions*
  - Wall squats
  - Wall presses (tricep extensions against wall)
  - Chest pulls
    - With elastic band

X-Factor: Cissus Quadrangularis

A medicinal plant from India, this supplement is mainly used for joint repair (pg. 186). Ferriss found himself using **both CQ and PAGG at the same time.** The **result was anti-fat gain and increased muscle growth effects.** This supplement hasn't been researched for long-term effects, so don't overuse it. The 4HB recommends **no more than 7.2 grams per day.** Continuous use is also not advised. Instead, use it every so often during muscular growth cycles or when you've injured a joint. *Ask your physician before use.*

Inside The Microbiome: Balancing Bacteria for Fat Loss

Studies have shown that two types of bacteria have become more plentiful in the general populations' gut biomes over the years. Bacteroidetes and firmicutes are fat-absorbing bacteria. Lean people tend to have more bacteroidetes while obese people have mainly firmicutes bacteria. To "cultivate a healthier and fat-reducing gut," follow these tips:

1. *Get off Splenda*
   a. *Fake sugars have been shown to decrease the helpful bacteria in our stomachs*
2. *Go fermented*
   a. *Fermented foods have high amounts of healthy bacteria*
   b. *Examples of fermented foods:*
      i. Cheese
      ii. Japanese natto
      iii. Kfire
      iv. Kimchi (kimchee)
      v. Sauerkraut
      vi. Fermented fish
      vii. Unsweetened plain yogurt
      viii. Kombucha tea
3. *Consider probiotics and prebiotics*
   a. *Probiotics: bacteria*
   b. *Prebiotics: fermented substrates that help bacteria grow*
      i. Contain organic inulin and fructo oligosaccharides (FOS)
         1. Not insulinemic
         2. Promotes calcium absorption

                        a. Promotes contraction-
                            dependent GLUT-4
            ii. *Examples:*
                1. Garlic
                2. Leeks
                3. Chicory
    c. *Provides beneficial effects against:*
        i. Allergies
        ii. Aging
        iii. Obesity
        iv. Other diseases
    d. *Increases serotonin*
        i. 95% of serotonin found in the gut
        ii. Effective alternative to treat depression

The Four Horsemen of Fat Loss

PAGG: A more sustainable supplement stack for fat loss.

Before: ECA

Ephedrine hydrochloride, caffeine, and aspirin (ECA) were *a popular stack of ingredients used for fat loss. The price for the rewards was unbearable side effects.* Severe headaches will begin quickly after cessation. Stimulant addiction can also form, making people continuously use ECA or find other drugs that are just as strong. High doses of stimulants in high-heat environments have been associated with heart attacks and death. The adrenal function will become lopsided, needing extra supplementation of stimulants to help with everyday function. *This is not a sustainable approach to fat loss.*

Ephedrine hydrochloride: 20 mg

Caffeine: 200 mg
Aspirin: 85 mg

After: PAGG

Policosanol: 20-25 mg
Alpha-lipoic acid: 100-300 mg (depending on personal tolerance)
Green tea flavanols (decaffeinated w/ at least 325 mg EGCG): 325 mg
Garlic extract: at least 200 mg

Tips:
- *Before breakfast: AGG*
- *Before lunch: AGG*
- *Before dinner: AGG*
- *Before bed: PAG (omit green tea extract)*
- *AGG is PAGG minus the policosanol*
- *Follow this 6 days a week*
  - Take one day off each week
  - Take one week off every two months* (Critical)

(P)olicosanol

Ferriss found a positive side effect of policosanol to be *body fat reduction*. Using the extract before bed with PAGG has a far superior effect in reducing body fat than that of AGG alone. After testing, the author concluded that *23 milligrams of policosanol a day is optimal* for this effect. Higher doses showed no additional benefits.

(A)lpha-lipoic acid (ALA)

ALA recruits GLUT-4 glucose transporters and takes it to muscle, not fat. This action increases insulin sensitivity and allows muscles to take the calories. In turn, fewer calories will be stored as fat. ALA is barely toxic to humans with its toxicity level being extremely hard to reach. *300-900 milligrams is recommended per day.*

(G)reen tea flavanols (EGCG)

EGCG also recruits GLUT-4 in muscle cells while simultaneously inhibiting GLUT-4 recruitment in fat cells. The recommended dose is *325 mg three to four times a day*. Getting to the 900-1,100 mg range per day will result in a sharp increase in fat loss. Try to *find decaffeinated green tea extract pills* to avoid illness from excess caffeine. Consult your physician before taking EGCG.

(G)arlic extract (allicin potential, S-Allyl cysteine)

Garlic extract contains high levels of allicin. This molecule has the surprising effect of *inhibiting fat regain.* This finding is due to its *combination with S-Allyl cysteine (alliin)*. Without it, allicin would putter out and not work because of the exposure to stomach acid. *Aged garlic extract (AGE) is recommended* for its high allicin potential and inclusion of S-Allyl cysteine. Unaged garlic extract will work the same but at a higher dose (pg. 202).

WARNINGS

PAGG has blood-thinning compounds, so consult your physician before using PAGG. You must have a constant consumption of B-complex while using PAGG. Do not use it if pregnant or breastfeeding.

Key Points:

- A low-carb diet can result in insufficient calorie intake, EAT CALORIES just not in the form of carbohydrates.
- Electrolytes will help replenish your body because of the excess water loss from the diet.
- It is best to indulge in one binge day a week rather than skipping it. Planned binging is better than unplanned.
- Working out more than 2-3 times per week could set back your progress.
- You want your meals to either leave your body as fast as possible or enter your muscles.

Back To You:

1. The Slow-Carb Diet is the main subject of this chapter. It is imperative to follow the diet exactly as stated, or the results won't be as effective. What are the five rules of the diet?

    1.

    2.

    3.

    4.

    5.

2. Because you aren't eating carbohydrates, you will lose excess water. What are the three electrolytes recommended to supplement the diet? Also, list three whole food examples for each one.

1.

    a.

    b.

    c.

2.

    a.

    b.

    c.

3.

    a.

    b.

    c.

3. It is normal for people to hit a plateau during this diet. What are the eight common mistakes that cause this plateau?

1.

2.

3.

4.

5.

6.

7.

8.

4. During binging, the main objective is to minimize how much of the "junk" food enters your bloodstream. List the three strategies that will prevent fat gain during binge days.

1.

2.

3.

5. PAGG is a supplement stack that Ferriss constructed. It is a sustainable additive to the Slow-Carb Diet. What are the four supplements that make up PAGG? List the recommended daily dosage of each.

1. P-
   a. Daily dose:

2. A-
   a. Daily dose:

3. G-
   a. Daily dose:

4. G-
   a. Daily dose:

Chapter 5: Subtracting Fat: Advanced

Ice Age

Mastering Temperature to Manipulate Weight

Michael Phelps consumes 12,000 calories daily. That isn't a typo. Technically, Michael would have to swim for ten hours straight a day to burn that many calories. So how does it work? He swims, and water has a thermal load 24 times more than air (pg. 207). *** This added temperature burns calories fast.*** Using temperature to your advantage, you can find that extra trick to get you to your end goal quicker.

From NASA to Everest: Correcting the Metabolism Equation

Weight loss or gain = calories in - calories out
- o   Wt = kcal in - kcal out

The main caloric expenditure shown is through activity level alone. However, thermodynamics is being left out of this equation. You can ***change your energy expenditure in three ways***:

1. Work (exercise)
2. Heat
3. Matter (excretion)

It Gets Better – The Devil is in the Details

One of Ferriss' colleagues showed impressive fat loss results while using cold exposure. Following a different diet and exercise plan, he lost 1.48 pounds weekly. Once *cold exposure* was added, he lost 4.77 pounds weekly in only six weeks. That's *61% more fat loss in half the time* (pg. 210).

Geek's Advantage: Fat-Burning Fat

There are two types of fat:

1. White adipose tissue (WAT)
2. Brown adipose tissue (BAT)

BAT cells are associated with muscle tissue and help disperse excess calories as heat. If they aren't dissipated, the calories would be stored as WAT fat. *Cold can stimulate BAT cells to burn glucose and fat as heat.*

[Ferriss' Experience]

Ferriss conducted personal research on himself and found a protocol that would activate
the BAT cells:

1. *Apply an ice pack on the back of the neck and upper trapezius*
   a. For 30 minutes
   b. In the evening

Research has shown that BAT cells are present in adults' necks and upper chests.

Ice Age Revisited – Four Places to Start

Four options have been formed to use cold therapy for fat loss:

1. *Ice pack on the back of the upper trapezius or neck*
   a. 20-30 minutes
   b. In the evening
      i. Insulin is at its lowest
2. *Drink 500 milliliters of ice water*
   a. On an empty stomach
   b. As soon as you wake up
   c. It increases the metabolic rate
      i. Peaks 40-60 minutes after drinking
   d. Eat the Slow-Carb Diet 20-30 minutes after
3. *Cold showers*
   a. 5-10 minutes long
   b. Before breakfast OR before bed
   c. Use hot water for the first 1-2 minutes
   d. Turn to cold and focus on the head and neck first
   e. Keep the water on your lower neck and upper back
      i. 1-3 minutes
4. *20-minute cold baths**
   a. *For high-tolerance individuals
   b. Induce shivering (safely)

    c. For EXTRA effect:
        i. Consume 200-450 mg of cayenne
        ii. 30 minutes before
        iii. With 10-20 grams of protein
            1. Not on an empty stomach

Six Reasons to Take a Cold Shower
1. **Fatty acid release**
   a. *Shivering recruits:*
      i. GLUT-4 in muscle cells
      ii. Heat production from physical shivering
2. **Increase adiponectin levels and glucose uptake by muscles**
   a. *Sugar is taken by muscle cells, not fat cells*
3. **Stimulation of BAT thermogenesis**
   a. *When there is no shivering*
4. **Improves immunity**
   a. *Immunostimulating effects*
      i. Pre-heat with warm shower or exercise
      ii. Increase in norepinephrine
5. **Effective against depression**
   a. *Shower at 68 °F for 2-3 minutes*
6. **Visible results of fat loss**

The Glucose Switch

Beautiful Number 100

Two Months Earlier – Firefly Restaurant, San Francisco

The company **DexCom produces glucose monitors** for diabetic individuals. **However, what if you could use this monitor as your body's gauge?** You could see the effects from certain meals, predict increased glucose levels, and schedule exercise based on it.

Making a (Wish) List... And Checking It Twice

Glycemic Index (GI) and Glycemic Load (GL): display how much specific foods raise blood sugar.

The higher these numbers are, the more blood sugar that will be in the body and be stored as fat. **Using a glucose monitor could indicate your own personal GI and GL,** which you could use to inform your decisions rather than guess off the "one-size-fits-all" research (pg. 226).

The Results

After testing his blood glucose for four straight days, Ferriss compiled a few noteworthy observations:

1. It's not when you put it in your mouth that counts. It's when it gets to the cells.

Food and drink take longer to enter the bloodstream than most would assume. A pre-gym snack for energy is worthless 20 minutes before your workout because it could hit your bloodstream an hour after you're done. *Eat everything an hour earlier for energy.*

For those post-workout protein shakes, the 30-minute window after completion is not ideal. *Drinking the protein an hour and a half before the workout, then consuming a major meal after the workout* works much better to get the protein to the muscles.

2. **Increasing fat content in meals blunts jumps in glucose much more than lean protein.**

For a decreased glycemic response, eat more fat and do it earlier in the meal (pg. 236). Eating healthy fat as an appetizer will do the trick.
- Brazil nuts
- One tablespoon of almond butter

3. **Fructose has a large and very extended glucose-lowering effect, but this doesn't mean you should consume it. Low blood glucose does not always equal more fat loss.**

Fructose has been shown to decrease blood glucose, but it will stall fat loss at the same time. *It is important to not just watch blood glucose levels and see the bigger picture,* especially if the goal is fat loss.

4. **Vinegar, counter to expectations, didn't lower glycemic response. Lemon juice, also counter to expectations, did.**

20 milliliters of vinegar with at least 5% acetic acid will work in lowering glycemic index (pg. 238). However, Ferriss experimented and found no effect. He concluded that a higher dose of vinegar is needed to affect fructose metabolism.

Lemon was tested and proved to lower blood sugar peaks by 10%:

- 3 tablespoons of *fresh-squeezed* lemon juice
  - No preservatives or artificial flavoring
- Before eating

5. **Cinnamon, even in small doses, has a substantial effect on glucose levels.**
   2.8 grams of cinnamon (1 ½ teaspoons) per day can lower the glycemic index by 29% (pg. 239). Cinnamon has multiple benefits:

   - Lower blood glucose
   - Lower LDL cholesterol
   - Lower triglycerides

   Cinnamon slows the rate at which food exits the stomach, making you feel full faster (pg. 239). The 4HB tested and ranked the *three types of cinnamon from most to least effective:*
   1. Saigon cinnamon
   2. Cassia cinnamon
   3. Ceylon cinnamon

The 4HB also ranked *methods of using cinnamon from most to least effective for decreasing glycemic index:*

1. Get fresh cinnamon that is grounded, or you can grind it yourself.
    a. Replace your spices and get new raw ones

2. Learn how to spot species.
    a. Cinnamon is not required to be labeled in the U.S.
    b. Cassia
        i. Rolls up on both sides
            1. Ex: a scroll
        ii. Darker reddish-brown powder
    c. Ceylon
        i. Rolls up on one side
            1. Ex: a bathroom towel
        ii. Lighter tan powder

3. Don't use too much
    a. Coumarin cinnamon is a blood thinner
    b. Use no more than 4 grams a day

6. **More than quality, it's the size and speed of meals that determine glycemic response.**

To decrease glucose spikes, there are *four strategies to decrease the amount of food you digest per minute:*

1. *Finish your plate in "thirds"*
   a. Wait five minutes between thirds
   b. Meals should take no less than 30 minutes
2. *Drink more water*
   a. Dilutes digestion
3. *Eat smaller portions*
4. *Chew more*
   a. Chewing each mouthful 20 times
   b. Counting slows down eating

7. **For the fastest fat loss, minimize your blood sugar bumps above 100 to no more than two per day.**

   Remaining under 100 mg/dL sustains rapid fat loss (pg. 242). This excludes binge days, and fructose shouldn't be used on non-binge days. Some rules to follow with the Slow-Carb Diet:

   - *Eat quantities of fat at each large meal*
     - Saturated fat is ok
       - For untreated meat
   - *Lunch and dinner should take at least 30 minutes to eat*
   - *Experiment with cinnamon and lemon juice before or during meals*
   - *Go to "Damage Control" for accidental binges*

The Last Mile

Losing the Final 5-10 Pounds

There is one effective strategy for losing an easy 5-10 pounds. **The main objective is to eat lots of protein.** Each meal should have a minimum of 4 ounces of protein in it. For every 10 pounds of lean muscle an individual has, they will adjust their ounces of protein intake. Examples of this ratio:

- 200-pound male (10-12% body fat) = 8 ounces of protein
- 190 pound = 7 ounces
- 210 pounds = 9 ounces
- For under 150 pounds = use the lowest level of 4 ounces of protein

The rules for this diet are as follows:

- One of these protein meals must be eaten every 3 hours while you're awake
- You must eat within 1 hour of waking
- You must eat within one hour before bed
- You cannot skip meals (you should not feel hungry)

To make it easy, here are some **meal options to eat every three hours:**

1. 50 grams of whey protein isolate + ½ a cup of nuts OR 2 tablespoons of peanut butter

2. 8 ounces of cooked, white, non-fatty fish (no salmon, mackerel, etc.) + ½ a cup of nuts OR 2 tablespoons of peanut butter

     a. Acceptable fish: catfish, lean tuna, white fish, pike, bass, whiting, flounder

3. 8 ounces of chicken or cooked turkey + 1/2 cup of nuts OR 2 tablespoons of peanut butter

4. 8 ounces of cooked protein that is fatty: red meat, ground beef, dark poultry or fatty fish + 1 macadamia oil OR a tablespoon of olive oil

5. 5 whole eggs (hard-boiled is easiest)

Here are more options of foods you are allowed to **eat unlimited quantities of at each meal**:

- Spinach
- Asparagus
- Brussels sprouts
- Kale
- Collard greens
- Broccoli rabe
- Broccoli and other cruciferous vegetables

More tips:

- *1 tablespoon of olive oil or macadamia nut oil for dressing*
    - Can't have if you already had peanut butter or nuts in that meal
    - Lower fat meals: 2 tablespoons olive oil or 2 tablespoons macadamia oil

- *NO corn, beans, tomatoes, or carrots*

Key Points:

- Using cold and heat therapies can manipulate your metabolism to burn more calories
- Cold showers are effective in burning BAT cells and recruiting GLUT-4 cells in muscle
- Increasing healthy fat foods can blunt blood glucose spikes
- Lemon juice and cinnamon have effective and desirable results on blood glucose levels
- Decrease the amount of food you're eating per minute… SLOW DOWN

Back To You

1. The author mentions the importance of thermodynamics in the metabolism equation. What are the three factors that influence a person's thermodynamics?

    1.

    2.

    3.

2. Burning fat is the main objective of this chapter. What are the two different types of fat, and which one is

associated with muscle cells? Why is this type of fat most desirable to burn?

1.

2.

Why is _____ fat more desirable to burn?

3. The author of The 4HB found interesting connections when he continuously tested his glycemic index. What are the seven observations that he found related to blood glucose levels? Highlight at least 3 of these findings.

1.

2.

3.

4.

5.

6.

7.

4. Controlling your glycemic response can decrease the amount of glucose being released by the body and limit the amount that turns into fat. What are the four methods of slowing down during meals that you can implement when you eat?

1.

2.

3.

4.

5. Losing that last 5-10 pounds of unwanted body fat is a difficult task. However, Ferriss has found an effective strategy of timed and portioned protein that will do the trick. There are given ratios of body weight to protein intake to follow during this diet. How much protein should you be eating based on your body weight?

Chapter 6 Adding Muscle

Building The Perfect Posterior

(Or Losing 100+ Pounds)

This chapter's main focus is on strengthening the posterior chain for both men and women.

Michelle Obama's Arms

For one of Ferriss' friends, Tracy, losing 100 pounds in 12 weeks was achieved because of one simple exercise: the Russian kettlebell swing. Tracy lost this much weight by doing kettlebell swings twice a week for 35 minutes maximum.

From Jiu-Jitsu to New Zealand: The Kettlebell Swing

Kettlebells became Ferriss' newest addiction for fast lean muscle. The instructions he was given were to *keep adding weight and reps to the swings* (pg. 265). A layout of his weekly workout routine looked like this:

Day 1 (Monday)

- High-rep kettlebell swings / 53 lb KB / MINIMUM 75 reps
- Slow myotatic crunch / with MAX weight / 10-15 SLOW reps

Day 2 (Wednesday)

- 3 sets x 5 reps each / 2-minute rest between sets
  - Iso-lateral dumbbell (DB) incline bench press
  - "Yates" bent rows / with EZ bar / palms-up grip, bent at waist 20-30 degrees
- Reverse "drag" curls / with thick bar / 2 sets x 6 reps / 3 min. rest between sets

Day 3 (Friday)

- High-rep kettlebell swings / 53 lb KB / MINIMUM 75 reps
- Slow myotatic crunch / with MAX weight / 12-15 reps
- ADD IN (every other week) / single-arm (SA) kettlebell swings / MINIMUM 25 reps per side

Guidelines for two-arm kettlebell swings:

- Stand with feet outside shoulder length about 6-12 inches
- Each foot should be pointed outward ~30 degrees
- Keep shoulders pulled back (retracted)
- Avoid rounding your back
- Backswing (lowering movement)
  - Sit back in a chair movement
  - NOT squat
- Don't let your shoulders go in front of your knees at all
- Forward swing (popping forward)
  - Pinch butt cheeks together tightly

The Minimal Effective Dose- How to Lose 3% Body Fat in One Hour a Month

For more ideas, here is an example of a prescription diet and exercise regimen. This prescription was specific to a female client who wanted to *lose the last bit of obnoxious fat*.

1. ***Breakfast switched to high-protein***
   a. 30% protein
   b. Ex: spinach, black beans, and egg whites with cayenne pepper flakes

2. ***Three exercises are done BEFORE breakfast***
   a. Two-legged glute activation raises / 20 reps
   b. Flying dogs / 15 reps each side
   c. Kettlebell swings / 20-25 reps

Learning The Swing

The kettlebell swing is an effective exercise when done properly, so it is critical to perform the reps well to optimize your results.

1. ***Touch-and-Go Deadlifts from Point A (3 sets x 5 reps)***
   a. KB directly between feet
   b. Bend down and perform deadlifts
      i. Head up, eyes straight ahead
   c. Once warmed up to the movement, perform touch-and-go's
      i. Make the movement more explosive on pick-up
   d. Touch the same spot on the ground every time

2. *Touch-and-Go Deadlifts from Point B (3 sets x 5 reps)*
    a. Repeat the deadlifts from above, but place the KB further back between the feet
        i. The spot on the ground should be in line with the heels
    b. When pushing hips forward, there will be more momentum

3. *Swings from Point C (sets of 10 reps)*
    a. Point C is the highest point where you can explode the kettlebell up
        i. End point: both arms straight at about chin height
    b. When first beginning, use a small swing to get momentum
        i. Then make the swings larger

Two-legged glute activation raises: pull your toes up as you drive off your heels

- Laying on the floor on your back
- Both knees bent

Flying dog: opposite arms and legs, right arm and left arm extend and vice versa to alternate

- On hands and knees on the ground
- Raise your arm and opposite leg up and straight

Critical (M)Ass: The Kiwi's Complete A/B Workout

You can never run out of posterior chain strengthening programs. By focusing on the back, you'll gain a more stable posture and stronger power. The "Kiwi" recommends 3-4 circuits of these exercises, however, Ferriss believes the MED is 2 circuits. *Perform "Workout A" on Monday and "Workout B" on Friday with glute activation raises performed before each.*

Workout A

> x 10 repetitions (13 reps max, so use heavier weight if you can do more)

1. Heavy dumbbell (DB) front squat to press
   a. Ass to heels
   b. Squeeze glutes at the bottom for one second
2. One-arm, one-leg DB row
3. Walking lunges w/ sprinter knee raise
4. Wide-grip push-ups

5. Two-arm kettlebell swings / x20-25 reps

Workout B

1. One-leg Romanian deadlift (RDL) / x10-12 reps
2. Chin-up / x10 or until you can't control the descent
   a. 4-second negative lowering
3. One-leg hamstring curls on Swiss ball / x6-12 reps
4. Front and side planks for abs / x 30 seconds
   a. Side planks for gluteus medius / x 30 seconds each side
5. Reverse hyper / x 15-25 reps

Six-Minute Abs

Two Exercises That Actually Work

Single White Male Seeking Abdominals: Exploring the Path Less Traveled

Conventional ab exercises only produce visible abs so well. The general population is not blessed with a high metabolism like most influencers, so why continually do these exercises over and over? Diet is often the determining factor for visible abs, but here are two ab movements that produce results.

1. *The Myotatic Crunch*

Benefits:
- Leverages the fully stretched position (stretch reflex)
- Uses full range of motion (ROM)
- Takes 3 weeks to see a difference

Steps:

1. Use a BOSU, Swiss ball, or pile of firm cushions
    o Lay on back on the ground with butt lifted off the ground
2. Arms stretched overhead
    o Keep arms behind or next to ears the entire time
3. Lower arms under control for 4 seconds
    o Until fingers touch the ground
    o Extend hands further away from the ball
4. Pause at the bottom for 2 seconds
    o Try to become as long as possible
5. Rise under control and pause at a fully contracted position for 2 seconds
    o Arms should not pass perpendicular to the ground

6. 10 repetitions
   o Add weight if 10 reps is easy
   o Don't go over 10 pounds of extra weight

2. ***The Cat Vomit Exercise***

Benefits:
- Targets the transverse abdominis (TVA)
  o Deepest abdominal muscle

Steps:

1. Begin on all fours
2. Keep your eyes looking under your head (at the ground) or slightly ahead of you (also on the ground)
3. Don't arch your back or strain your neck
4. Forcefully exhale
   o Until all air is out
   o Abs should be contracted at this point
5. Hold your breath and pull your belly button up toward your spine
   o Do this as hard as you can for 8-12 seconds
6. Inhale fully through the nose after the hold
7. Take one breath cycle of rest
   o Exhale slowly out the mouth
   o Inhale slowly through the nose
8. 10 repetitions

Square is not feminine: preserving the hourglass

Maintaining an hourglass figure is difficult for a female. Becoming a square is easy. This usually occurs when using progressive resistance exercises. Some exercises that will maintain the hourglass instead are:

1. Timed planks
    i. Front planks (30 seconds)
    ii. Side planks (30 seconds each side)
2. Hip flexor stretches
    i. Hold for 30 seconds in each position
    ii. Fixes pelvic tilt

From Geek to Freak

How to Gain 34 Pounds in 28 Days

Prelude: On Being Genetically Screwed

You can be predisposed to gaining muscle mass more easily. The specific gene that causes this growth is the ACTN3 gene. *It targets proteins for fast-twitch muscles, which in turn has the most potential for growth* (pg. 295).

How Did I Do It?

Ferriss was able to gain 34 pounds of muscle in 4 weeks. His routine:

Morning

- NO-Xplode (2 scoops)
- Slo-Niacin (or timed-release niacinamide, 500 mg)

Each Meal

- ChromeMate (chromium polynicotinate, not picolinate, 200 mg)
- Alpha-lipoic (200 mg)

Pre-workout

- BodyQUICK (2 capsules 30 mins. Prior)

Post-workout

- Micellean (30 g micellar casein protein)

Prior to Bed:

- Policosanol (23 mg)
- ChromeMate (200 mcg)
- Alpha-lipoic acid (200 mg)
- Slo-Niacin (500 mg)

The four simple principles to follow to optimize growth:

1. ***Perform one set-to-failure for each exercise***
   a. Total time under tension: 8-120 seconds per exercise
   b. 3-minute rest between exercises

2. ***Use a 5/5 rep cadence***
   a. 5 seconds up – 5 seconds down
   b. Eliminates momentum

3. ***Focus on 2-10 exercises per workout, no more.***
   a. Include at least one multi-joint exercise
      i. Pressing
      ii. Pulling
      iii. Leg movements
   b. Example of one workout ("+" means superset, aka no rest in between):
      i. Pullover + Yates's bent row
      ii. Shoulder width leg press
      iii. Pec-deck + weight dips
      iv. Leg curl
      v. Reverse thick-bar curl
      vi. Seated calf raises
      vii. Manual neck resistance
      viii. Machine crunches

4. ***Increase recovery time along with size***

a. Occam's Protocol

The Colorado Experiment: 63 Pounds in 28 Days?

The Colorado experiment was an extensive research project focused on minimalist training. The finding is that you can **gain muscle mass without spending a lot of time in the gym**. Workout sessions lasted an average of 33.6 minutes. It is noted that this experiment has faced criticism for multiple unaccounted factors. Although the actual workout consisted of using extremely high weights, there is a simpler protocol that can be utilized:

1. Leg press x 20 reps
2. Leg extension x 20 reps
3. Squats x 20 reps
   a. Increase weight by 20 pounds at the 20-rep mark
   b. Then work back up to 20 reps

TWO MINUTE REST

4. Leg curl x 12 reps
5. Calf raises 3 sets x 15 reps
6. Behind-neck pull-down x 10 reps
7. Row x 10 reps
8. Behind-neck pull-down x 10 reps

TWO MINUTE REST

9. Lateral raise x 8 reps
10. Press behind-the-neck x 10 reps

TWO MINUTE REST

11. Curl x 8 reps
12. Underhand chin plus weight for reps

TWO MINUTE REST

13. Tricep extension x 22 reps
14. Dips x 22 reps

The Myth of 30 Grams

Recommended protein daily intake is 0.8-2.5 grams per kilogram of body weight (pg.311). The 4HB recommends *1.25 grams per pound of current lean body weight for muscle gain.* To find this number you must subtract your body fat from your total fat.

Occam's Protocol I

A Minimalist Approach to Mass

The Bike-Shed Effect

The main idea: don't listen to others. Ferriss describes this effect as people saying they know it all without having any real knowledge of the subject. Nobody knows how to build a nuclear power plant, but everyone says they could build a bike shed to the smallest detail (pg. 315). This is not true.

Complicate to Profit, Minimize to Grow

The diet and exercise industry makes money by complicating things. This keeps people coming back for more help. The 4HB is a minimalist novel; to grow is to stay simple (pg. 316).

Objectives the 4HB will NOT achieve for you in this chapter:

1. *Won't make you a professional athlete*
2. *Won't make you as strong as possible (that's in "Effortless Superhuman")*

The main objective of this chapter is to trigger specific muscle growth with as little effort as possible.

Even though this program preaches minimalism, safety is always at the forefront of concern. No matter how easy the exercise is, if it's not done properly, it will set you back more than push you forward. ***Your priorities for exercise performance should be as follows:***

1. *Reduce injury potential*
2. *THEN increase performance*

Occam's Protocol

Guidelines:

- *Alternate between workouts A and B*
- *Each exercise should be performed for only ONE set to failure*
  - You want to fail
  - 5/5 cadence
    - Abdominal exercises and kettlebell swings are the only exceptions to cadence
- *Want to stimulate local and systemic growth*
  - Longer time under tension (TUT) will accomplish this
- *Keep shoulders in "locked position"*
  - Protect your shoulder health
  - Pull shoulder blades back and down towards hips

Workout A: Machines

1. Close-grip supinated pull-down x 7 reps (5/5 count)

2. Machine shoulder press x 7 reps (5/5)
   a. Record seating settings on all machine exercises
   b. Optional: abdominal exercise from "Six-Minute Abs"

Workout B: Machines

1. Slight incline/decline bench press x 7 reps (5/5)
   a. No more than 20 degrees incline or decline

2. Leg press x 10 reps (5/5)
   a. Optional: kettlebell or T-Bar swings x 50 ("Building the Perfect Posterior)

3. Stationary bike x 3 minutes at 85+ rpm

Workout A: Free Weight

1. Yates row w/ EZ bar or barbell x 7 reps (5/5)

2. Shoulder-width barbell overhead press x 7 reps (5/5)
   a. Optional: abdominal exercises from "Six Minute Abs"
   b. Keep elbows in front of shoulders (not flared outward)
   c. Bar travels in front of the face
   d. Head and upper torso move forward under the bar
   e. A split stance prevents arching of the back

Workout B: Free Weight

1. Slight incline bench press with shoulder-width grip x 7 reps (5/5)
   a. No Power Rack = use dumbbells

2. Squat x 10 reps (5/5)
   a. Optional: kettlebell or T-Bar swings x50 ("Building the Perfect Posterior")
   b. Feet slightly shoulder-width
   c. "Break your hips", imagine pouring water out the front of your pelvis
   d. Then, sit backward

3. Stationary bike x 3 minutes

Rules to Lift By

1. *Adding weight*
   a. If you can complete the minimum amount of repetitions, increase the weight by 10 pounds
   b. If this is still easy after a few reps, take a 5-minute break and add another 5-10 pounds
   c. Hit set to failure

2. *Dropping weight*
   a. Don't drop weight when you hit failure
   b. Attempt to move the weight slowly and carefully as much as you possibly can
   c. Once attempted you can drop the weight
   d. If you feel like you can do another set a minute later, you didn't hit failure

3. *Don't pause at the bottom or the top*
   a. EXCEPT for the bench press
   b. Take 3-minute breaks between all exercises

4. ***Weight and repetitions change, not other variables***
    a. Everything should be identical in each workout
        i. Ex: rep speed, exercise form, rest time

5. ***Don't add exercises***
    a. The temptation will be there, trust the protocol

Occam's Frequency

The frequency of workouts will decrease as weight increases.

It takes longer for the body to recover a 20-pound muscle than a 10-pound muscle you had a month ago (pg. 328). Sessions should be scheduled by the number of rest days, not set days (ex: Tuesday, Thursday). ***The space between each workout will increase as you progress.***

Getting Started

1. Take AT LEAST 7 days off all training that causes significant muscle damage (soreness).

2. Start with 2 days between workouts A and B
    a. After two of both workouts, increase rest days to 3 days
    b. If an exercise stalls at all, increase the rest days to 4 days
    c. EAT ENOUGH CALORIES

Occam's Feeding

When it comes to trying to consume all these calories, people's appetites differ. Some individuals can eat a lot of food less frequently while others have to eat less more frequently. Finding which routine suits you will make eating second nature, not forced.

If you're prone to skipping meals, ingesting enough calories is key. Protein shakes and bars are calorie-dense and can easily be utilized throughout the day.

Night Owl Calorie-Dense Meal Schedule:

> 10:00 AM- Wake up and breakfast (+ ½ shake)
>
> 2:00 PM- Lunch
>
> 6:00 PM- First dinner
>
> 7:30 PM- Training (sip on low-fat protein)
>
> 8:30 PM- (30 min. post-training) Dinner
>
> 15 minutes before bed- Second half of morning shake

Supplemental Calorie Meal Schedule:

> 9:00 AM- Protein shake
>
> 11:00 AM- Protein bar
>
> 1:00 PM- High protein/carb lunch
>
> 3:00 PM- Protein bar
>
> 5:00 PM- High protein/carb dinner
>
> 7:00 PM- Protein bar
>
> 9:00 PM- Protein snack with carbs
>
> 11:00 PM- Protein shake

A Note on Skipping Breakfast

If you find yourself skipping breakfast, use the blender for shakes!

Meal replacement/ pre-bed snack:

- 24 oz (3 cups) 2% or whole milk
- 30g whey protein isolate (chocolate is usually better)
- 1 banana
- 3 heavy tbsp almond butter
    - No added sugar, maltodextrin, or syrups
- 5 ice cubes

Total calories: 970 cal., 75g protein

The Fixer: GOMAD

GOMAD = Gallon Of Milk A Day

Adding one gallon of **organic milk a day has been shown to accelerate an increase in muscle gain**. The fat gain will also ensue, it's normal, but be sure to keep track of it. However, if you have an easier time with the weight gain, you can change GOMAD to LOMAD (liter) per day instead. The liters can be incorporated in shakes or just a plain glass of organic milk.

Occam's Prescriptions

The protocol can be successful supplement-free. However, there are a few suggested supplements if you can afford them.

1. Cissus quadrangularis- 2,400 mg, 3 times per day
2. Alpha-lipoic acid- 300 mg, 30 minutes before each whole-food meal

3. L-glutamine- 10 g, every 2 hours (80 g a day)
    a. Used for tissue and intestinal repair
4. Creatine monohydrate- 3.5 g in the morning and before bed, 5-6 g a day if you use a powder form
    a. Used for maximal force production and protein synthesis (pg. 335)

Occam's Protocol II

The Finer Points

Common Questions and Criticisms

Can this frequency really be enough?

Muscle repair is one of the slowest tissue repairs in the body. Other wounds or trauma could take 8-12 hours or 1-2 days. *Muscular damage is much slower and optimal training frequency is no more than once a week* (pg. 347).

How do I determine starting weights?

Use trial and error, but safely. Start with only 5 reps for each exercise with a minute rest between each. If you can complete more than 5 reps take a minute break and add 10% weight or 10 pounds (whichever is lowest). Once you get up to a weight where you fail to complete the 5 reps stop. *Take 70% of the final weight and that's your starting weight to use.* For shoulder presses use 60% of the final weight.

How do I add weight?

If you complete the minimum reps, add 10 pounds or 10% of the weight. To maintain this progress, you NEED to eat a disgusting amount of calories.

What if I miss a workout due to travel?

Free weights and Olympic barbells are universal in weight rooms. If you can become accustomed to them, it's recommended to use them. However, *it's better to take one to three days off than train inconsistently*. Using unfamiliar equipment is not helpful for your progress.

What if I don't make the target number of repetitions?

There are two reasons as to why this happened:

    1. insufficient failure during the last workout

    2. insufficient food/rest

If you finish 6 out of 7 good reps then keep working out. If you can't even complete 6/7 then go home immediately. Take the next day off too, it's mandatory. *Don't drop the weight and try again, just stop.*

How many calories should I consume?

Adding the protein shakes and milk should help gain weight and thus make counting calories unnecessary. On the flip side, if you aren't gaining weight then count and track calories for 24 hours. You should be eating around 20 calories for 10 pounds more than your lean body weight (pg. 351). Overall, *if you're not adding weight, eat more.*

But what about cardio?

Improving the muscular system's strength will in turn improve your cardiovascular system. If you are a marathoner or a runner then you will need to add aerobics. Most people are noncompetitive athletes looking to stay healthy. *This program will provide better cardiovascular health naturally.*

What if I'm an athlete?

It depends on the sport, but in general you need to design a specific program for you. "Effortless Superhuman" may be more accurate for increasing your training. *Frequent sports training is still important.*

Won't this speed of lifting make me slow?

This program is not made for athletes specifically. This program is designed around a 5/5 cadence and although the tempo may seem slow, *there is no evidence proving that this will cause you to decrease speed* (pg.353).

What about warm-ups?

Use *60% of your working weight at a 1/ 2 cadence before each exercise*. Three reps will suffice to warm the targeted muscles up before working.

How should I work out with a partner?

Don't let your partner get in the way of your "gains." Your rest intervals need to be exactly 3 minutes and shouldn't be altered because your partner wants to talk. These exercises are also safe to do alone, so don't let your partner try to "spot" you on your failure sets.

What about drop sets, rest-pause, and otherwise extending failure?

If you cannot move the weight any more then you have past failure. Doing anymore will just waste resources needed to grow (pg.354).

Isn't X better than Y? Can I [insert change to protocol]?

If you need anything more than gaining weight then get a different program. This program is strictly for gaining weight and doesn't need any modifications.

Can I just work out every 12 or 24 days as Guru X suggests? I'm still getting stronger.

That is a different objective to the Occam Protocol. This program is designed to focus on tissue growth. To achieve this, you must support high rates of fat-free growth (pg. 355).

Doing the least possible to experience strength gains (training infrequently) vs. *Doing the least necessary to maximize size gain* (Occam Protocol)

What to do if your gains slow with one session per week?

Try splitting up your workouts so you aren't doing a total body every session. This will increase GLUT-4 windows to at least two times per week. An example of this is:

Session 1: Pushing exercises

- Incline bench press
- Dips (add weight)
- Shoulder-width grip shoulder press (never behind the neck)

Session 2: Pulling exercises

- Pullover
- Bent row
- Close-grip supinated pull-downs
- SLOW shrugs with dumbbells (pause for 2 seconds at the top)

Session 3: Leg exercises

- Leg press with feet shoulder-width

- Adduction machine
- Hamstring curl
- Leg extension
- Seated calf raise

Key Points

- Kettlebell swings are very beneficial and should be your posterior's new best friend.

- Targeting the deep abdominal muscles will produce aesthetic results.

- Focused exercise can activate ACTN-3 genes and will provide protein to fast-twitch muscles for growth.

- For muscle gain, the recommended daily protein intake is 1.25 grams per pound of current lean body weight.

- If you're stalling in progress, you're either not resting enough or not eating enough.

Back To You

1. Learning about tissue growth is essential when it comes to adding weight. The 4HB states four principles that explain how to maximize efforts to stimulate tissue growth. What are the four simple principles to optimize growth?

A)

B)

C)

D)

2. Find your daily amount of protein for muscle growth. Using the numbers you collected, subtract your body fat from your body weight. Take that number and multiply it by 1.25g.

Total fat = Body weight - total fat

Total fat x 1.25 (grams) = daily protein intake

3. In "Rules to Lift By," baselines are stated on knowing when to add weight. Explain when you should add weight to an exercise.

4. Get to know yourself. In "Occam's Feeding," the subject of meal timing is focused on. Every individual eats differently, when do you find yourself eating in a day? State the approximate times that you perform the following actions. Insert or remove actions that you do regularly. This will give you a layout to determine if you can eat a small amount of high-calorie meals a day or if you should eat multiple small meals instead.

Wake up:

Breakfast:

Snack:

Lunch:

Snack:

Dinner:

Snack:

Go to bed:

5. Adding milk, protein shakes, and protein bars to your diet will help you get the calories you need. With that, there are multiple different brands of all three foods. Do some research and find two brands/types of each of the following. Fill out the related information for each brand.

Organic Milk

Brand-

    Price-

    Where to buy-

    Calories-

Brand-

    Price-

    Where to buy-

    Calories-

Protein

Brand-

Price-

Where to buy-

Protein per serving-

Brand-

Price-

Where to buy-

Protein per serving-

Protein Bars

Brand-

Price-

Where to buy-

Protein per serving-

Brand-

Price-

Where to buy-

Protein per serving-

Chapter 7 Improving Sex

The 15-Minute Female Orgasm

Part Un

Nina and 400 Hollywood Nights

The 4HB has compiled as much research on the female orgasm as possible. Pulling information from the world-renowned Nina Hartley, Ferriss wanted to highlight these two objectives:

1. The single most important precondition needed for female orgasm
2. Technical modifications of positions

The precondition: women need to step up to the starting line first

The woman needs to be comfortable with themselves orgasming first.

It is difficult for a partner to induce that sensation in the woman if she is not in a comfortable state of feeling that way. There cannot be unwarranted guilt or shame associated with orgasms (pg. 369). There are *a few tips to begin this positive process:*

- Start in small increments by yourself

- 5 minutes a night before bed
- Immediately when you wake up
- Listen to self-talk

The positions: precision and pressure

Two small modifications can be made to sex positions:

1. **Changing the angle** of penetration. The penis can be angled up toward the woman's G-spot. This area is 1-2 inches inside the vagina and upward. Taking the index finger up to the second knuckle, make a "come here" motion, and the fingertip should press against a sponge-like tissue (pg. 370).

2. **Changing the pressure** of positions. Positioning the partner's pelvic bone in direct contact with the clitoris will add extra stimulus for the woman.

Improved-Angle Missionary

Tips:
- *A firm pillow*
  - To elevate the woman's hips and tilt towards her head
- *Partner's hips should be as close as possible to the woman's*
  - The lower they keep their hips the better
- *Experiment with penetration rhythm*
  - A few short lengths with one long
- *For longer strokes:*

- "Open up" one hip
- Put her bellybutton at the twelve o'clock position
- Aim for either ten or two o'clock
- *Woman's positioning to elevate her hips*
  - Pull her knees toward her chest
  - OR place feet flat on the bed

Improved-Pressure Missionary

Tips:

- *Partner must shift their weight forward*
- Bring legs closer together and straighten them
  - This puts more weight on the woman's pelvis
    - Pressure on the clitoris, not the vaginal wall
- Aka pelvic grinding
  - Rock the hips back and forth in a small motion
  - Move hips side to side or in small circles slowly

Conventional Cowgirl Position vs Improved-Pressure Cowgirl Position

Tips:

- *Partner's body position*
  - NOT laying down OR sitting straight up
  - Should be leaning back 20 degrees

- Use a pillow to support the back
- Use an armless chair
- *Partner provides pressure, the woman provides movement*
  - Apply consistent pressure
  - When in doubt: have her do the movements

Part Deux

Stupid Animals

More often than not, the man usually finds himself **confused about where to put his hands**. It's common and difficult to find if you're not educated. That's why The 4HB is here to guide you through the anatomy.

Clitoral Confusion

The clitoris or the "clit" can be imagined as an upside-down "V" with its sides extending down to wrap around the vaginal opening (pg. 379). The "g-spot" stimulation is technically stimulation of the crura (sides of the "V") and *orgasms overall originate from stimulating the clitoris.*

Clitoral Confidence

Upper-left quadrant sensitivity on the clitoris could be a possible cheat code.

8,000 Nerve Endings and Two Sheets of Paper

Tips:
- *Go by how it feels, not by the sounds (pg. 382)*
- *Pressure should be about two sheets of paper worth*
- *During manual stimulation*
    - The forearm should be parallel to the woman's body

A more useful definition of orgasm

Orgasm can be defined as: involuntary contractions from a single point of contact of the clitoris. There can be no resistance, physically or mentally, when it comes to orgasms. Comfort is key.

The Practice and How-To: The 15-Minute Orgasm

Ferriss has found that to become proficient at giving orgasms, you must practice. Ultimately, these tips are recommended for partners open to direct communication about goals. There are three recommendations on how to practice:

1. Explain to your partner that it is a goalless practice.

Goalless as in no expectations. ***To become good at this you must practice without worry of obligation to achieve.*** The woman isn't expected to provide any sort of effort except for mindful focus on the exercise.

2. **Get into position.**

   01. Woman gets into a comfortable position
      a. Laying on back with neck supported by a pillow
      b. Legs bent and spread
         i.   Can support hips with a pillow
   02. Using the left-hand
      a. Sit on her right side
      b. Straddle bent left leg across her torso
         i.   Use pillows for support
   03. Using right hand
      a. Sit on her left side
      b. Slightly tilt your wrist for a better finger angle

3. **Set the timer for 15 minutes, find the upper-quadrant point of greatest sensation, and stroke.**

15 minutes is the limit. ***This makes the activity a "focused repetition" not a goal with performance pressure.***

Here is a detailed ***step-by-step guide to finding the upper quadrant and anchoring***:

01. Separate the labia
02. Retract the clitoral hood upward
      a. With the heel of the palm
03. Anchor the clitoris with the right thumb
      a. You must hold the hood back
04. Put left hand under buttocks (anchor)
      a. Two fingers under each cheek

    b. Thumb resting on (not in) base of entrance of the vagina

05. *Clitoris is at "twelve o'clock"*
    a. Go to around "one o'clock" with the right index finger
    b. Stroke LIGHTLY
    c. Only very small movements
        i.   1/16 of an inch width of movement
    d. The tip of the finger is better than the pad
        i.   Cut and file fingernails before

06. *Use a constant speed for 2-3 minutes*
    a. Stay consistent and then change speeds for another 2-3 minutes

07. *The elbow-brace position*
    a. Used for when the partner's lower back is agitated
    b. The left elbow is braced on the left shin
    c. Have to use your left hand to immobilize her right leg now

08. *Grounding*
    a. Signals the finish of the exercise
    b. Helps the woman ease out and disconnect from the activity
    c. Apply strong pressure on the pubic bone
        i.   Up toward her head
        ii.   Use overlapping hands

Suggestions for a Successful Beginner's Session
Tips:
- *Light contact*

- No more than two pieces of paper as the depth of pressure
- *Keep the practice goalless and only 15 minutes*
  - Intentional focused repetition
- *Use a blindfold or eye mask for the woman*
  - Helps with comfort levels
  - Increases tactile sensitivity
- *"Turn off the show"*
  - The woman doesn't need to please you
  - She doesn't need to add any flourish
- *Make it fun*
  - Serious = unwanted tension
- *NO idle chatter*
  - Keep from unnecessary talk
    - This can be distracting from the exercise
    - Use the eye mask to take away embarrassment
- *Reinforce relaxation*
  - The woman should be completely relaxed
  - If she's having strong contractions:
    - Breathe and push out slightly

Most Common Mistakes:

- *Being goal-oriented*
  - Don't give in until the 15 minutes is done
  - You can indulge after
- *Asking "nonwinning" questions*
  - Don't ask questions like "Does it feel good?" or "Are you enjoying this?"
    - She will feel pressured to lie
  - Ask directional questions:

- "Would you like lighter or stronger strokes?"
- "More to the left or right?"
- "Higher or lower?"
- *Using too much pressure*
  - It must be the lightest touch possible
  - Ex: tickling a sleeping friend's nose without waking them up

Extra Strategies After Mastering: The Basics
- *Insert the middle finger*
  - Of the non-stroking hand
  - Use the "come here" motion
    - Locate the g-spot
  - Add a second finger after 5 minutes and continue the motion
- *Use a firm pillow under her hips and left thumb to anchor the clitoris*
  - Perform the strokes at the "one o'clock" upper quadrant
    - Lightly
  - After 5 minutes, add finger insertion with the right hand

Sex Machine I

The Death of the Metrosexual: Reclaiming Aggression
How could one lose interest in sex? It's possible and more common than most people care to admit. Ferriss goes into detail about the possible problems one might be experiencing that create this disinterest.

Possible short circuits

Testosterone is produced from multiple chain reactions:

Hypothalamus releases GnRH → pituitary gland releases LH and FSH → testicles produce testosterone

*GnRH- gonadotropin releasing hormone *LH- luteinizing hormone *FSH- follicle-stimulating hormone

Injecting external testosterone does not fix the problem that originates in that chain reaction. Plus, *low libido does NOT mean there is a low testosterone problem.*

Ferriss experimented with human chorionic gonadotropin (hCG). This luteinizing hormone increases seminal volume and low libido. *Constant use of this drug causes desensitization of the testes to real luteinizing hormone* and a decrease in the natural production of testosterone.

Geek's Advantage

Even though luteinizing hormone (LH) produces testosterone, testosterone is not the sole perpetrator for low sex drive. *LH is seen as the key to this problem even for females.* LH increases as a female's sex drive heightens right before ovulation.

My Solution: Two Protocols

These solutions are protocols that don't require needles or prescriptions. The first one is for long-term maintenance and the second is for short-term boosts, aka fun (pg.409).

Protocol #1: long-term and sustained

Fermented cod liver oil + vitamin-rich butter fat
- 2 capsules
  - Upon waking
  - AND before bed

Vitamin D3
- 3,000-5,000 IU
  - Upon waking
  - AND before bed
  - Reach blood levels of 55 ng/mL

Short ice baths and/or cold showers
- 10 minutes each
  - Upon waking
  - AND before bed

Brazil nuts
- 3 nuts
  - Upon waking
  - AND before bed

Protocol #2: short-term and fun "nitro boost"

800 milligrams of cholesterol
- Within 3 hours of bedtime
- Night BEFORE sex
- Ex: 4+ large whole eggs or yolks

4 hours before sex
- 4 brazil nuts

- 20 raw almonds
- 2 capsules of fermented cod/butter

SHBG-The Party Spoiler

Sex-hormone binding globulin (SHBG) is an antagonist to testosterone. It cancels out the effects by binding to testosterone. So even if you have a high testosterone count it can be scrapped by SHBG. However, cholesterol has been shown to block out SHBG from binding. By restricting SHBG from binding to testosterone, there are more free (unbonded) testosterone available. *This makes cholesterol our friend in short-term testosterone boosting.*

Happy Endings and Doubling Sperm Count
Unpleasant Surprises

Viable sperm in males has decreased drastically over the years.

There are millions of possible reasons why this might be true, however, The 4HB dives into cell phone use as the main perpetrator. When evaluating sperm, doctors look at three variables:

1. How many there are in **total.**
2. How many have proper **morphology** (shape).
3. How many can swim forward in the right direction **(motility)**?

Happy Endings

Ferriss follows this simple protocol for eleven weeks:

- *The phone stayed in an armband, not in his pocket*
- *If in a pocket, the phone was turned off completely*
- *Alternative: phone in backpack or bag*

The results of these new precautions with additional cold treatments and supplemental selenium tripled his motile sperm (pg. 424).

The Reasons to Store Sperm

1. Men are becoming progressively infertile.
   a. Unfriendly testicle foods and toxins are at an all-time high

2. Medical conditions can render men infertile.

3. Sometimes you change your mind about whether you want kids.
   a. As you get older you might want children of your own
   b. Reversal vasectomy procedures have a high failure rate

4. Why not?
   a. The downside to doing it is recoverable (cost)
   b. The downside of NOT doing it is irreversible

Sperm Storage- The Steps in Brief

1. *Find a sperm storage facility*

2. *Make an initial appointment to get tested*
   a. Required testing for common STDs
   b. Initial consult price: $100-150
   c. STD lab panel price: $150-200

3. *It takes six sessions for the chance at one kid*
   a. Abstain from ejaculation for at least 48 hours before each session
   b. Cost per sample frozen: $150-200 (x6 = $900-1,200 per kid)

4. *Store all sperm somewhere safe*
   a. Cost per year for storage: $300-600

Key Points

- For a female to orgasm, she must first feel comfortable physically and mentally.
- The upper left quadrant of the clitoris could be a useful sensitivity that some women may have.
- Increasing luteinizing hormone (LH) can increase an individual's libido.
- Decreasing phone contact with testicles has been shown to increase fertile sperm count.
- It is advantageous to store sperm just to be prepared for what the future may hold for us.

Back To You

1. The 4HB covers the steps to please women in bed. Multiple adjustments are offered to help a female reach orgasm. What are the two main modifications that can be made to sex positions?

A)

B)

2. Orgasms are the main topic of this chapter. What is the definition of an orgasm?

3. It is important to follow the successful tips to better practice inducing an orgasm. However, it is critical to be aware of the common mistakes. What are the three common mistakes seen when practicing a "15-minute orgasm?"

A)

B)

C)

4. The author provides a short-term dietary plan to temporarily increase testosterone. One of the diet's contents is to increase cholesterol. We learned that cholesterol can help increase testosterone. Referring to "SHBG- The Party Spoiler," explain how cholesterol makes more free testosterone?

5. The action of storing sperm is emphasized in this chapter. Ferriss touches on the topic that we don't know what the future has in store for us, so better to be safe than sorry. What are the 4 reasons to store sperm?

A)

B)

C)

D)

Chapter 8: Perfecting Sleep

Chapter 8 discusses several methods Tim Ferriss has used to gain a good night's sleep. Some work better than others. He found different things had an impact on different levels of sleep.

Engineering the Perfect Night's Sleep

Insomnia is a horrific combination of internal monologue and various yoga-type positions. At one time, Ferriss had **terrible insomnia**. After trying many remedies, Tim finally found relief.

Hidden Third of Life

Bad sleep is caused by one of these problems:
- Takes too long to fall asleep
- Wake up often during the night
- Wake up and cannot get back to sleep

To get some answers, the crucial questions to answer about sleep are:
- What is the amount of REM I get?
- What is the amount of delta-wave sleep I get?
- Do I have sleep apnea?

To answer these crucial questions, Tim felt he could not go to a sleep lab and get the correct data. He needed a pocket-sized lab.

My First F*cking Sleep Lab

Brad Feld had what Tim needed to measure his sleep without going to a lab.

Of Motion and Waves: The Tools

Brad's tool was Zeo, a new, next-generation sleep tool. During months of testing, Tim used various devices, including Zeo, WakeMate, FitBit, glucose monitors, movement detection monitors, etc., to **gather data**.

Tim's findings included the following:

- The amount of deep sleep in a night directly affects the productivity of one's sleep. When more REM sleep happens during the night's sleep, the more positive the impact on the sleeper.
- Tim could increase the amount of sleep by either extending sleep past 9 hours a night or waking himself four plus hours after going to sleep for five minutes.
- Taking huperzine-A 200 micrograms before going to sleep increased the amount of sleep. Huperzine-A is a good extract used before as a learning accelerator and to increase lucid dreaming.
- The more deep sleep you have, the more your physical performance increases. Deep sleep repairs tissues and strengthens your immune system.
- Drinking wine less than four hours before bed lowers deep sleep. However, wine consumed more than six hours before did not have an effect. Time is crucial.

- Putting butter made from almonds on celery before going to sleep eliminates bad waking-up feelings by half. This helps to increase the repair of cells and lower tiredness and fatigue. Oil from flaxseed can be added, but the taste and smell could be better.

Turning Off the Monkey Mind

Tim changed his lifestyle and the tools he used to **find a way to sleep faster**. Tim did not include any drugs in the testing. It had to work at minimum three consecutive nights for something to succeed.

- Room temperature at night. Tim found that 67-70 degrees was the best temperature for him to fall asleep. However, everyone is different, so each person needs to experiment to find the correct temperature for them.
- Eating a big protein and fat filled meal at least three hours before sleep. For example, four eggs which can provide 800 mg (milligram) of fat/cholesterol and 40 g (grams) of lean protein cause a strong sleepiness effect.
- Philips GoLITE. Using the goLITE for 15 minutes is very useful. The long battery life and small size make it easy to use anywhere.
- Iso-lateral movements help exhaust the nervous system. There were effective results with doing one arm and one leg stabilization exercises.
- Take a cold bath one hour before bed. Taking a short ten-minute ice bath with or without a small

dose of melatonin one hour before bedtime shortens the time it takes to go to sleep.

- Use an ultrasonic humidifier. Tim recommends the Air-O-Swiss Cool Mist Humidifier for best results. The humidifier works exceptionally well with the goLITE.
- Use a Nightwave Pulse Light. The soft blue, pulsing light emitted into the darkened bedroom helps to synchronize your breathing and slows it to bring you to sleep faster.
- Resort to the Half Military Crawl position. This is to be used as a last resort. The position locks you in so you cannot move. Less tossing, turning, and fidgeting brings faster sleep.

Tools and Tricks

Tim lists several websites of tools he used to speed up going to sleep time.

- Becoming Uberman
- Sleeping Less with Polyphasic Sleep

To go without any sleep for long periods of time is nearly impossible. Tim has found ways to **break sleep into multiple sections**, equaling two hours of total sleep, and still performs tasks successfully. These approaches are illustrated with personal stories.

Enter Dustin Curtis

Dustin sought solutions for his non-24-hour sleep schedule, which did not sync with everyone else.

Hello, Polyphasic Sleep

In **polyphasic sleep**, the belief is that the most beneficial sleep is REM sleep. Normal sleepers only have one or two hours of deep sleep during the night. Polyphasic sleepers need to increase the REM time during the night for best results while shortening the time in actual sleep. REM sleep happens faster if the body is conditioned to have shorter sleep times.

Methods to obtain Polyphasic Sleep:
- The "Siesta" method includes one 20-minute nap during the day and a large chunk of sleep at night. Adding one nap daily takes away an hour and 40 minutes of total sleep needed in 24 hours.
- The "Everyman" method contains different combinations of 20-minute naps and core sleep. The sleeper needs to experiment with different combinations to find the best one for them.
- The "Uberman" method has six evenly spaced 20-minute naps and no core sleep. Total sleep time is 2 hours in 24 hours.
- The Catch
- In the Everyman and Uberman methods, a strict schedule must be followed. You cannot oversleep or miss a nap! The new sleep routine should be set in two to three weeks.

Uberman 101

Step 1: Determine your sleep schedule.

- Take 20-minute naps every four hours, every 24 hours. This cycle stays the same throughout the polyphasic sleeping period.

Step 2: DO NOT oversleep.

- Naps must be only 20 minutes. Oversleeping once will upset the cycle and result in exhaustion. Get a reliable alarm to use.

Step 3: DO NOT skip naps.

- Skipping one nap will upset the cycle. There will be a loss of energy that will need two additional naps before a return to mental sharpness.

Step 4: Beat the initiation phase.

- The first week and a half are the toughest. Stick to the schedule, don't oversleep, and don't skip any naps! You should be on your new polyphasic sleep routine in two weeks, although it might take up to three weeks.

Tools and Tricks

Tim lists websites of tools and personal statements used in the Becoming Uberman section of the chapter.

Key Points

- The higher the percentage of REM during sleep, the more the ability to recall skills and data from the past 24 hours increases.

- Average sleepers get approximately two hours of REM during a night's sleep.
- Deep sleep is essential in repairing tissues and strengthening the immune system.
- Room temperature, high protein and fat meal at dinner, blue-light emitter, iso-lateral exercises, an ice bath before bed, ultrasonic humidifier, and a nightwave pulse light all induce faster sleep.
- Polyphasic sleep can be achieved with a strict schedule.
- Sleeping a total of two hours in 24 hours can be achieved using the "Uberman" method of polyphasic sleep.

Action Plan
- Understand the type of insomnia you have - taking too long to fall asleep, waking up throughout the night, or waking too early and not being able to go back to sleep - and use tools or methods to address that condition.
- If you cannot fall asleep easily, select one of the tools given to help achieve this goal. Select only one and follow the instructions for a few days to decide if it is effective for you.
- If one of the tools does not generate the desired effect, try a different method.
- Utilize one of the non-drug polyphasic methods to decrease the amount of time you sleep at night while still feeling refreshed when you awake.
- Remember that for the tool or method to be effective, it must be followed and achieve the desired impact for consecutive days.

Chapter 9: Reversing Injuries

Chapter 9 follows Tim Ferriss' attempts to reverse lifetime injuries through different strategies. He describes the therapies, exercises, and tools that most successfully worked for him.

Reversing "Permanent" Injuries

In June 2009, Tim questioned if he could **reverse his lifetime injuries and physical abuse** in 14 days. He was able to accomplish the reversal in six months.

The $10,000 Lesson

Tim's first attempt to reverse his injuries was a series of injections of a variety of chemicals and medications. The injections consisted of:

- Platelet-rich plasma (PRP) is a treatment used with elite athletes. PRP contains the plasma portion of your blood with concentrated platelets. This is the base to which other medications were added.
- Stem cell factor (SCF) which assists in blood cell production.
- Bone morphogenic protein7 (BMP-7) helps adult stem cells develop into bone cartilage.
- Insulin-like growth factor 1 (IGF-1) is one of the most potent natural cell growth and multiplication activators—a drug used in professional bodybuilding.

The result was that the doctor could see **no real difference before and after MRIs**.

The Reason

Tim tried the expensive and painful route to help heal his numerous fractures, tears, and other lifetime injuries. However, the **injections and prescriptions did nothing more than mask his symptoms**. After the last injection, which left Tim in a drug-induced haze, he determined to fix his problem with measures he developed himself.

The Menu

Tim developed a four-stage approach to address lifetime injuries.
- #1 - Movement: Focus on correct posture movement of the body.
- #2 - Manipulation: Use aids or pressure with your hands to fix tissue damage.
- #3 - Medication: Use shots, supplements, or ointments.
- #4 - Reconstruction: Surgery

When using this routine, you only go to the next stage when one fails. Surgery is the last resort. Sometimes, it is possible not just to restore but exceed previous capabilities.

There are numerous movements, manipulations, and medications listed which are effective. Most helped, but the relief did not last for more than 48 hours or could not be performed alone. However, six treatments reversed "permanent" injuries.

1. Shoe Heel Removal and Vibram Training. Area Fixed: Lower Back. Wearing shoes with elevated heels creates painful posture curvature. The result is a posture that is both hunchbacked and swaybacked simultaneously. Tim recommends Vibram Five Finger and Terra Plana shoes by Vivobarefoot, which have erased his lower back pain for the first time in ten years.

2. The Egoscue Method. Area Fixed: Cervical/Neck and Mid-Back. Named for inventor Peter Egoscue, also called "supine groin progressive," was discovered accidentally. Although this has proven inconvenient and time-consuming, Ferriss has found it to be the most effective tool in relieving hip flexor, pelvis, and hamstring tightness.

Step-by-step directions and diagrams are included in the six exercises used in The Egoscue Method.

1. Static Back (duration 5 minutes)
2. Static Extension Positions on Elbows (duration 1 minute)
3. Shoulder Bridge with Pillow (duration 1 minute)
4. Active Bridge with Pillow
5. Supine Groin- Progressive Stretch using Tower (duration 50 minutes)

Supine Groin (Alternative by using chair)

1. Use an Air Bench (duration 2 minutes)

2. AMIT- Advanced Muscle-Integration Therapy. Fixes: Multiple areas including Glutes, Pectorals, and Calves. Craig Buhler's muscle therapy is very effective in treating tight or painful muscles and how the nervous system turns muscles on and off. His treatment is of the muscles that have taken over for the muscle that has deactivated because of the overload or stress. After trying multiple treatment therapies, Tim found the work with the objective weights to have the most striking results.
3. Active-Release Technique, also known as ART. Fixes: Internal shoulder rotators.
   a. This method, developed by Dr. P. Michael Leahy, is to shorten the tissue, apply tension, and then lengthen the tissue. It is literally wrenching muscles apart from the outside to remove adhesions and restrictions.
4. Prolotherapy. Fixes: Left-side knee and right-side wrist. A mixture of irritants, such as "sugar water," is injected into tendons, ligaments, and inside joints to create a mild inflammatory response that stimulates tissue repair.
5. Biopuncture. Fixes: The Achilles Tendon. Biopuncture is the shallow injection of multiple tiny needles into the facia. It is a web of connecting tissue that binds muscles together to break down calcium deposits where they should not be. The results are awe-inspiring with minimal downside.

Tools and Tricks

Tim suggests focusing on **practitioners treating patients before 2010** to guard against con artists and self-proclaimed experts.

Tim lists several websites for information on the people and products used in this chapter.

How to Pay for a Beach Vacation with One Hospital Visit

An Introduction to Medical Tourism

Tim discusses **medical tourism** agencies and the opportunities for medical procedures in foreign countries, such as Nicaragua. The amount of money saved by not using facilities in the United States more than paid for his luxurious two-week vacation.

As Easy as 1, 2, 3

In a Nicaragua emergency room, Tim had a multitude of tests and procedures, including numerous MRIs, urinalysis, blood tests, and several X-rays, to utilize when he was back in the States getting treatment for his residual pain. He would use these as reference tools for future therapies. Hospitals in the United States seldom do multiple reference tests or imaging because of insurance company concerns. Besides the convenience of having these tests and images, the **differences in cost and treatment of the patient** between the foreign hospital and one in the United States are immense.

Tools and Tricks

Tim lists websites helpful in planning a medical vacation.

Pre-Hab Injury-Proofing the Body

This is a difficult section of the chapter but the most important for most readers. The small upfront investment of time allows for faster progress without serious setbacks. The emphasis is on **injury prevention through different movements**.

Gray's Anatomy: From the NFL to Special Ops

Injury-proof your body using the 80/20 principle.

80/20 Functional Screening

According to Gray, **injury results from imbalance**. A self-assessment, scored as pass or fail, can be used to identify left-right imbalances and motor control issues:
- Squatting deeply
- Stepping over a hurdle
- Lunging inline
- Raising a straight leg
- Rotate in a seated position

The Critical Four

The first step is to isolate the problems with FMS. The second step is using corrective actions. Of the many actions to take for correction, Gray stated the **critical four actions** are:

- C&L- The Chop and a lift
- TGU- The Turkish Get-Up
- 2SDL- Deadlift with both arms
- 1SDL- Deadlift across the body with one leg

The listed exercises should be learned and done according to the order show below:

The Critical Four Schedule: Finding and Fixing

Tim provides the schedule he used to find and fix his imbalances.

Coordination
It is not a workout but a session to practice the movements. Practice with no weights until movement can be performed on both sides, then add light weights.

Testing
Test to find your least strong quadrant and weakest sides— one week.

Fixing
After identifying the imbalances, perform the above exercises in each workout. There are detailed directions for each exercise and a progression to the next.

- Sets and Reps: For all exercises for weeks 2-6, use a 2:5 ratio of sets for strong and weak sides and a repetition of 3-5.

Optional Weeks 7+
Exercises and schedule provided for sustained pre-hab and strengthening.

Exercise Details

Tim provides detailed descriptions and pictures for the Critical Four movements.

Exercise #1 - Chop and Lift (C&L)

- Half-Kneeling Description addresses upper and lower asymmetries
- The 80/20 Chopping and Lifting Program Guidelines
- Stick with a "bar" for the first month or two
- Unload between repetitions if possible (rest the weight stack)
- Single-Leg Flexibility Assessment- Test to assess the imbalance of sides
- Options- to obtain the proper position without lifting the weight stack
- Don't Hold Your Breath
- Make Your Positioning 100% Consistent Workout to Workout
- Hand Positioning
- Head and Shoulder Rotation

Let the Testing Begin

After testing all four quadrants with the C&L movements, the goal is to identify the weakest quadrant. Directions are given for the C&L procedure and how to test. You **test to the point of loss of appropriate posture and smooth movement or to the point that it is a struggle** to complete the movement. Although it is not required, having someone watch you or record the movements is helpful.

Exercise #2 - The Turkish Get-Up (TGU)

The TGU is complex and should be viewed as a long-term exercise. A low-weight warm-up should be practiced for a few minutes before each workout. It includes nine different movements that address all major muscle groups and movements.

Extensive directions and pictures are provided to guide the reader through the corrective exercise.

Exercise #3, #4 - Deadlift across the body with one leg (1SDL)

The deep muscles in the hips are stabilizers as much as movers. This exercise makes left-right imbalance obvious.

- Learning with the Two-Arm Single-Leg Deadlift (2SDL), the 1SDL is used in training, but it is good to become comfortable using two arms that create a better balance. A diagram and instructions are included.

- Performing the One-Arm, Single-Leg Deadlift
  Extensive directions on performing 1SDL are given.
- Deadlift Guidelines from Gray
  1. The deadlift looks like a forward-bending motion, but it is really a sitting-back motion.
  2. Keep the grip strong to keep your shoulders safe.
  3. Fully extend and straighten the back leg.
  4. Lift a respectable amount of weight.

The deadlift is designed to keep repetitions low, causing neuromuscular reactions that create core stability.

Tools and Tricks
Tim includes numerous websites that provide information on different materials in the Pre-Hab section of the book.

Key Points
- Tim becomes a "guinea pig" to discover if it is possible to reverse life-long injuries.
- Tim goes through a series of injections of medications with no noticeable improvements.
- Tim designs a four-stage program to address lifelong injuries. Movement, manipulation, and medication brought relief, but it did not last long. Surgery is the last resort.
- Six treatments cause permanent relief from lifelong injury/pain. Each treatment treats a different area of the body.

- Tim describes a medical vacation to Nicaragua, where the pricing and how patients are treated are superior to United States hospitals.
- It is advisable to use the exercises and movements in this chapter to prevent injuries before they happen.

Action Plan

- If you experience a long-lasting injury, consider using the movement, manipulation, and medication parts of the four-stage program. Only consider surgery as a last resort.
- Determine which area of your body is impacted by the permanent pain from injury.
- Use a combination of the six treatments that provide needed relief.
- In anticipation of tests or images that you might need for treatment, after extensive research, consider going to a foreign hospital for better pricing.
- Consider using Tim's program to prevent injuries before they occur.

_____

_____

_____

_____

_____

_____

_____

Chapter 10: Running Faster and Farther

This chapter discusses Tim's attempts to achieve physical excellence in the NFL. Many short, personal stories of different peoples' experiences using the programs are also discussed.

Hacking the NFL Combine I

Preliminaries - Jumping Higher
The introduction to the chapter shows that whatever works is what is used/done.

The Science and Business of Running Faster

Ferriss visits trainer Joe DeFranco, known for the unbelievable achievements of the men he has trained for the NFL Combine. Ferriss wanted to see if he could **improve his vertical jump and 40-yard dash**.

The Vertical Jump

After Tim demonstrates his highest vertical jump – 22 inches – DeFranco's regimen begins by **focusing on improvements** needed.

- Flaw #1: Too Little Shoulder Drive
  The importance of using upper-body strength to increase the height achieved.
- Flaw #2: Pulling the Extended Arm Back at the Apex of the Jump

The arm used to mark the height needs to be
retracted on the jump going up.
- Flaw #3: Too Wide a Squat Stance
The feet need to be placed inside the hips
when squatting.

With these three simple changes, two inches were added to
the height of the next attempt of the vertical jump.

- Flaw #4: Tight Hip Flexors

Static stretching must be used to put the hip flexors asleep,
maximizing leg extension. After the static hip flexor
stretches for 30 seconds, the height of the next vertical
jump grew to 25 inches.

Tools and Tricks

Tim provides a list of websites for more information and
videos of superior vertical jumps.

Hacking the NFL Combine II

Running Faster

Joe DeFranco lists some experts who he considers the best
in their fields. Considering Joe's past accomplishments,
Tim hopes to **improve his sprint time**.

The Warm-Up

Pictures and descriptions of **a short warm-up mimic the good habits of sprinting**. The warm-up includes General Movement Prep, Ground-Based Dynamic Stretching and Muscle Activation, and Frequency Drilling to Prep the Nervous System. Then, there is a resting and recovery period before testing.

The Set-up

The same technology used in the Combine measured Tim's time. Tim's times were: Dash #1: 2.12 secs., Dash #2: 2.07, 40-yard dash: 5.54 secs. Not good times!

The Devil's in the Details
- Beginning with the first step to take in the sprint, The First Round of Positional Corrections provides five steps in correcting the first step—the improved training time on the next attempt 1.99 secs.
- The next step was Adding Correct Arm Position and Movement. In the first step, Tim's arms were positioned at a negative arm angle. He had to pause and lift his arm before the first step. He placed his shoulders slightly ahead of his fingers to correct this, driving his lead arm backward instead of lifting it. After practicing this approach, the time he clocked was 1.91 seconds.
- For Focusing on Sustained Running Position and Fewer Steps, Joe DeFranco prescribed four easy steps to follow in Tim's next attempt. The fifth attempt was down to 1.85 secs.

"Just Run Your 10"

Putting everything learned into play is essential in shortening the time in the 10-yard dash. Remembering everything he had learned, Tim's 40-yard dash attempt was 0.2 seconds faster. However, he needed to stop because his hamstring felt tight. When Tim looked up during his sprint, it pulled his torso up and **caused the hamstring to tighten**. Joe immediately stopped the session.

Hip Thrusts at the Coffee Shop: Preventing Hamstring Tears

Since hamstring pulls are so numerous, Joe has developed a pre-hab **prescription to help stop pulls from happening in the first place**.

- Train the natural glute-ham raise. A website is given to show proper form. According to Joe DeFranco, athletes who perform this movement seldom have hamstring pulls.
- Focus on hip extension strength. Five different movements were recommended to focus on strong hip extensions. They include the supine hip thrusts, which also give quick relief for back pain from sitting on a laptop too long. Two videos and pictures showing proper form are included in this section.
- Keep your hip flexors flexible. When hip flexors are tight, it creates tension, which causes tears. Flexible hip flexors are crucial in lengthening your stride.

Homeopathy: The Problem and Paradox of Arnica Montana 30c

Tim took **Boiron Arnica Montana** 30c pellets, which he found preferable to the liquid option of homeopathic medications. Possible explanations:

- Homeopathic Remedies Work as Advertised. The liquid actually retains some of the properties of the original substance.
- The Placebo Effect. The promise that the homeopathic remedy reduces pain causes the person taking the remedy to believe it is working.
- Regression Toward the Mean. The severity of symptoms worsens and then improves until you are back to normal. The body heals itself, but the homeopathic remedy is thought to be the reason for getting better.
- Some Unexplained Mechanisms. Science has not yet discovered the mechanism through which homeopathic medicines work.

Tools and Tricks

Tim provides websites and videos that further illustrate the Hacking the Combine section of the chapter.

Ultra-Endurance I

Achieving 5K to 50K (12 Weeks) - Phase I

Kelly Starrett catches Tim's attention by telling him **he prepared for a marathon by doing lots of 400-meter repeats**.

Two and a Half Weeks Later

Tim meets Brian MacKenzie, who promises he can get Tim to be able to do a **half marathon in eight weeks**, even though he has little experience in running long stretches.

The Journey from High Volume to Low Volume

As a triathlon and Ironman competitor, Brian had heavily trained up to 24 to 30 hours a week. Brian questioned the logic of the high-volume, low-speed aerobic training. He **adopted a training mix that reduced the time spent in training**.

So, You Want to be a Runner? Let's Try 400-Meter Repeats

Tim realized after a number of 400-meter and 100-meter repeats that he needed help in his training.

Preparation: The Undercarriage

After four weeks with several problems that would hinder long-distance running, Tim realized he needed good suspension.

Of Marathon Monks and Antelopes: The Enzymatic Equation

After muscle biopsies and lab work, Tertius Kohn, Ph.D., told Tim that long-distance running would be extremely difficult. Even after all of his training, his **enzyme levels were completely normal**. This meant that Tim's achievements would be attributed to his training.

Tim did **pre-training preparation** for four weeks. They included five movements and running. Pictures and descriptions of the five movements: Hip Flexor (Iliopsas) and Quad Flexibility, Pelvic Symmetry and Glute Flexibility, Repositioning the Pelvis, Pre-workout (Weight and Otherwise) Glute Activation and Strengthening of the Feet and Ankles are provided.

Becoming Biomechanically Efficient Technique (Form and Tempo)

Nicholas S Romanov, Ph.D., created the Pose convention for running. His five principles are:
- Lean forward and use gravity.
- Stay on the top part of your feet.
- Make sure not to straighten your legs.
- Pull your feet to your buttocks.
- Try to hold 180 steps per minute.

Running by the Numbers: Using Video to Capture Three Snapshots

The snapshots of the three trials of Tim's 400-meter repeat to **illustrate his stride** are included in this section. His running economy improved immensely. Tim found four things that helped him the most:

- Strive for 90 steps on each leg.
- Lean but fall like a tree instead of bending at the hips.
- For the pull off the ground, imagine pulling the heel up to the buttocks at a   45-degree forward angle instead of straight off the ground.
- Use minimal arm movement and consider keeping your wrist near your nipples the entire time.

Pose as Panacea: Careful with the Ankles

Tim warns that the Pose Method is **not for everyone**. Research shows that while Pose works spectacularly for some, many injuries can occur in others.

Ultra-Endurance II

Achieving 5K to 50K (in 12 Weeks) - Phase II

Tim states that you have to understand that **the body has limitations**. Only then can you overcome them. Strength training improves marathon time.

Moving the Aerobic Line

If you already have a sufficient aerobic base, **training should focus on getting you to remain in aerobic** and move at faster speeds. It can take six to eight weeks to move the line. Graphs help to explain what needs to be improved.

12 Weeks to 50K

Tim provides the exact 12-week program he used to move from 5K to 50K.

FAQ with Brian

Brian answers the following questions:
- What shoes are the best?
- The front of my shins kill me after running. How can I prevent this?
- Is there a simple indicator of bad form I can monitor while running?
- What should I do if I get fatigued during intervals and my form starts to fail?
- What type of diet do you follow while in training?
- Do you take anything in particular post-workout?

Forced Evolution

Was Tim able to become a 50K ultrarunner?
Race Feeding: Tips from Scott Jurek

The importance of training the body to process food during movement is discussed.

The Dean's List
Dean Karnazes lists his favorite marathons with websites included.

Can Six Minutes of Effort Improve an 18.6-Mile Test?
It has been shown that **short bursts** of all-out exercising can be as effective as long hours working out in the gym.

Tools and Tricks
Tim provides videos and websites for endurance workout tools.

Key Points
- Using the regime created by Joe DeFranco, Tim improved his vertical jump by 3 inches and his 40-yard dash by 0.33 seconds.
- It is essential to analyze and correct the flaws in your form to improve the vertical jump.
- For the warm-up for sprints, it is crucial to do sprints as many repetitions as possible.
- Correcting the runner's position on the first step, the arm position and movement while running, and taking fewer steps with the correct running position greatly improved sprint running times.
- Since hamstring injuries are very prevalent, it is important to condition to stop the injuries before they happen.

- It has been shown that short bursts of strenuous exercise are as effective as working at the gym for long periods.

Action Plan
- Even though you might not want to be in the NFL Combine, if you are an athlete, you definitely want to improve your performance.
- Decide which athletic performance addressed in this chapter you would like to improve.
- Once you have decided on the area of interest, follow the directions of the professionals.
- Do not be discouraged if your improvement is not immediate. Keep working!

_____

_____

_____

_____

_____

_____

_____

Chapter 11: Getting Stronger

In this chapter, Tim Ferriss discusses different techniques and methods he has used to become stronger.

Effortless Superhuman

Breaking World Records with Barry Ross
Not only is strength a skill but it can also be learned quickly.

Reducing the Irreducible
Ferriss explores Barry Ross' quest to find how to **make humans as fast as possible**. Tim cannot believe the improvement he has seen in strength.

The Effortless Superhuman Protocol
The protocol for a 17-year-old high school student that Barry Ross trained for 12 months is studied. She ultimately ran the fastest 200 meters in the world. She trained three times a week following this protocol:
- Intense stretching to start
- Either bench presses or push-ups with a five-minute rest
- Deadlift up to knees, at least 2 sets of 3 reps at 90%
- Core exercise: 3-5 sets of 3-5 reps (isometric holds)
- Static stretching

Muscle strength is important. All **other things being equal, the stronger runner will win**.

How to Perform the Conventional Deadlift
Photographs show Larry Lamar performing a conventional deadlift. A description of the protocol is also included.

The Basic Rule: Keep it less than 10 Seconds
Do not exceed 10 seconds of tension for exercise sets because you want to minimize lactic acid production. **Lactic acid can delay muscle repair.**

The New and Improved Trinity
Barry has narrowed his sprint-specific program to three training goals:
- Competition conditioning
- Maximal strength
- Maximal speed

Diagrams, pictures, and descriptions of each goal are provided.

The Sumo Deadlift
Barry uses the sumo deadlift instead of the conventional deadlift because the **pull distance is shorter, and the lower-back position is safer**. Photographs are provided to demonstrate the lift.

Maximal Speed
Once Barry's athletes are strong, he makes them faster. Barry's method is a sharp contrast to conventional methods.

The Rule of 10 Reps by Pavel Tsatsouline

The goal is to **build as much strength as possible** while staying as fresh as possible for your sport. It is important to remember to lift heavy weights but not make it hard. Stories of different athletes' experiences illustrate other strength training methods.

The Sharapova Sit-Up: Janda
The **Janda sit-up** is an abdominal exercise for power development without bulk. The "rule of 10 repetitions" is applied here. Pictures and descriptions of how to perform the sit-up are provided.

Timing Workouts: Using Chronobiology for Faster Gains
Chronobiology is the science of **investigating time-dependent changes in physiology**. When is the optimal time for you to train?

Tools and Tricks
Tim provides a list of websites to provide more information.

Eating the Elephant

How to Add 100 Pounds to Your Bench Press
Background of the Bench: My Achille's Heel
Because bench press had always been Tim's weakest exercise, he got help from Marty Gallagher, a renowned coach of powerlifters.

Enter Marty Gallagher

Marty designed a workout prescription for Tim or anyone who wants to add 100 pounds to their maximum lifting weight in six months.

There are three requirements:
- Requirement #1: A periodized tactical game plan. Progressive resistance pre-planning.
- Requirement #2: No missed workouts.
- Requirement #3: Adding a *significant* amount of muscular body weight.

A table of the 12-week bench press cycle was provided. The bench press will be trained once weekly, and you will train three grips in each session. **Protein must be kept high** to raise lean muscle mass: 200+ grams daily.

Now What? Alike Yet Different
After an athlete has completed a successful 12-week cycle, **gains need to be solidified**. The body needs 4-6 weeks to reset. Phase II and Phase III need to be done to add 100 pounds to your bench press in six months.

Phase II: Reestablish Homeostasis
Phase III: Assault on 300

Tools and Tricks
Tim provides websites, book and magazine suggestions, and interviews to give more information on powerlifting.

Bench Pressing 854 Pounds: Set-Up and Technique
Pictures and description of Mark Bell's form in bench pressing, which can be used to bench 500 pounds or less.

Key Points

- Not only is strength a skill, but it can also be learned quickly.
- Tim cannot believe the improvement he has seen in his strength using Barry Ross's techniques.
- Increasing strength has a direct effect on running speed.
- All things being equal, the stronger runner will win the race.
- The crucial principle of the Rule of 10 Reps is to lift heavy but not hard.

Action Plan

- If you want to increase your running speed, understand that building strength is key to achievement.
- Research Marty Gallagher's protocol for strength to see if it fits you and your lifestyle.
- If you are interested in the bench press, try the 12-week program that Marty Gallagher has developed.
- Once you have finished the 12-week cycle, solidify your gains after a resting period with Phase II and III.
- Spend some time looking at Tim's websites in Tricks and Tools.

Chapter 12: From Swimming to Swinging

In Chapter 12, Tim explains how he overcame his hatred for swimming and became an avid swimmer in two months.

How I Learned to Swim Effortlessly in 10 Days

After several different tries at various techniques to learn to swim, Chris Sacca shared an answer.

The Method

The method is **Total Immersion (TI)**. Tim used a book and DVD to become a swimmer! However, parts of the book are difficult to understand, so Tim has developed a list of tips.

My Eight Tips for Novices

1. Move forward with the least amount of effort, keep your body horizontal, and do not pull or kick your legs or arms.
2. Keep yourself horizontal by aligning your head with your spine - you should look straight down. A video is listed that helps you understand how to conserve energy.
3. In line with the video, swim freestyle on alternating sides to avoid the stomach.
4. Move through water with your fingers aimed down and extend your arm completely. It should always go lower and farther than you think.
5. Think about improving your arm stroke length (SL) instead of your arm stroke rate (SR).

6. Extend and stretch your arm underwater while turning your body – not your head – for breath.
7. Experiment with hand swapping as a drill.
8. Forget about workouts and focus on "practice."

Full descriptions and pictures accompany the tips.

Gear and Getting Started
Tim recommends the **best gear and pool** to start.
- Gents, don't swim in board shorts.
- Get good goggles.
- Start practicing in a pool that is short and shallow.

Hard to Believe
Tim learned to love swimming! He considers it to be **moving meditation**.

Tools and Tricks
Tim suggests videos and websites to help in learning and enjoying swimming.

The Architecture of Babe Ruth

Obsessive Batting Disorder (OBD)
Hitters improve their batting through the help of Jaime Cevallos.

From God to Granularity
Tim has Jaime use his expertise to turn him into a homerun hitter.

- Before-training average: 57.307 mph
- After-training (first round) average: 65.23 mph
- After-training (second round) average: 70.076 mph

The training focused on the following fundamental principles and exercises for 45 minutes to achieve this increase.

Picking the Angles

The Big Three
1. The Cushion
   a. The Cushion occurs when the front heel has landed before the swing.
2. The Slot
   a. The proper Slot position is when the back elbow drops to the player's side and the spine angle stays vertical.
3. Impact Position
   a. The Impact position is the thumbprint of the swing.

Pictures and descriptions are given on improving The Big Three by adjusting angles.

CSR (Cevallos Swing Rating) = 3(180-E) + W Two benefits of a high CSP swing:
1. A high CSR swing is naturally a tighter swing. Since the swing is closer to the torso, it forces the hitter into better pitch selections because he cannot swing at pitches outside the strike zone.
2. In a high CSR swing, contact with the ball is made further back, closer to the pitcher. This gives the

pitcher more time to assess the pitch before swinging.

Tables and diagrams are included to illustrate CSR.

Advanced Concepts (Important for live pitches)
Notice should be paid to Areas of Impact (AOI), indicating a hitter's level of consistency, and Angle L, which measures bat-lag – how late your bat comes through the strike zone.

Practicing Your Angles
Pictures and descriptions are given for the best drill to hone a new Impact position: to hit the impact bag, pause, and check the position.

Tools and Tricks
Tim lists books, websites, and tools that help improve your hitting.

Key Points
- Tim has a deathly fear of swimming, which, although he has tried to overcome, he finally has the tools to do so.
- Tim gives eight tips for new swimmers to follow when beginning to swim.
- Tim provides a list of gear needed to be successful when starting to swim.
- Jaime Carallos helps Tim improve his batting percentage by improving his swing.

- There are two benefits to using the swing Cevallos taught Tim. The swing is naturally tighter, and the contact with the ball is made closer to the catcher.

Action Plan
- If you fear swimming, utilize the tips and gear Tim gives in this chapter to learn to swim.
- Decide if you want to improve in baseball by hitting the ball harder and further.
- Follow the lessons that Jaime Carlos taught Tim to become the best.

_____

_____

_____

_____

_____

_____

_____

Chapter 13: On Longer and Better Life

Chapter 13 discusses different therapies and alternatives that can be used to lengthen life.

Living Forever

Vaccines, Bleeding, and Other Fun

Tim recounts a 20-year experiment on rhesus monkeys. One group is on a diet. The other group eats whatever they want. The group on the **calorie-restricted diet has a two-thirds lower death rate** than the other group.

However, the scientist observed two twin monkeys in the two different groups in the study. One scientist observed that the monkey on the low-calorie diet looks drawn, weary, and miserable. The monkey in the high-calorie group is a happy camper with sparkling eyes, glowing skin, and a laid-back attitude. **There is more to life than living a long one.**

Tim says the real question is: How can you **increase the length of my life without severely decreasing my quality** of life?

The Short List

Tim has developed a list of minimally inconvenient therapies that should work to **increase life expectancy**. However, he cautions that these therapies often do not have long-term human data, which could have unpredictable side effects.

- Resveratrol
- Injections of the immunosuppressant drug rapamycin
- Alzheimer's vaccines
- Stem cell therapies

A few alternatives that are low-cost, low-tech, and low-risk are provided. Most also provide athletic or body composition benefits.

1. Cycles of 5-10 Grams of Creatine Monohydrate (cost: $20/month)

     Popular among power athletes, it has also been shown to minimize or prevent Alzheimer's, Parkinson's, and Huntington's diseases. Complications are rare.

2. Intermittent Fasting (IF) and Protein Cycling (cost: Free)

     Several versions of IF and semi-IF protocols are listed, including Fast-5, ADCR, and Protein Cycling, with a sample menu and protein sources.

3. The Lost Art of Bleeding (cost: Free)

     Donating blood has positive implications for the donor.

A Little Flower, Please

Extending life at the expense of quality of life makes little sense.

Tools and Tricks

Tim provides websites for different ways to extend life, including blood donation, diets, and sites to put things in perspective.

Key Points

- Is it worth lengthening your life if you sacrifice the quality of life?
- Tim has developed a short list of therapies that should increase life expectancy, including Resveratrol, immunosuppressant drug rapamycin injections, Alzheimer's vaccines, and stem cell therapies.
- Tim lists low-cost alternatives, which also provide athletic benefits.
- Donating blood has a positive impact on the donor.

Action Plan

- Spend some time pondering if strict dieting is worth the impact it can make on your well-being.
- If you decide that dieting is the answer, consider a diet that is not overly strict.
- Try one of the low-cost, low-tech alternatives that Tim suggests to help prolong life.

Chapter 14: Closing Thoughts

Tim offers a few closing thoughts on some of the subjects covered in the book. He adds more information to supplement the book.

The Trojan Horse

Tim considers this book a Trojan Horse. He hopes that reading it has helped the reader connect the dots on the different subjects in this book. The side effect of making the physical changes is the incentive to continue. The book is intended to **make you a better all-around human**.

Partial Completeness

Most people resign themselves to *partial completeness,* usually through self-talk. Tim believes **the fastest way to improve your inner self is to improve your outer self**. The separation of mind and body is false. They are reciprocal.

Becoming Complete

Your body is almost always within your control. Controlling your body puts you in life's driver's seat.

Appendices and Extras

Charts of Helpful Measurements and Conversions

Getting Tested - From Nutrients to Muscle Fibers

A few guidelines include:
- Don't test it if you can't act on it or enjoy it.
- Take the same tests at the same time.

- If you get an alarming result, repeat the test before making significant changes.

The Menu
List of the tests discussed and the cost.

Muscles of the Body (Partial)
Diagram of a body showing the muscles.

The Value of Self-Experimentation
This chapter is written by Dr. Seth Roberts, who is the emeritus professor of psychology at the University of California-Berkley and professor of psychology at Tsinghua University.

Dr. Roberts relates his **experiences in self-experimentation** and what he learned from it.

He found three uses:
- To test ideas.
- To generate new ideas.
- To develop ideas.

He felt there are three advantages of self-experimentation over conventional research:
- More power.
- Stone Age-like treatments are easy to test.
- Better motivation.

Tools and Tricks

Tim provides a list of websites on self-experimentation and examining habits.

Spotting Bad Science 101

Scientists often change their minds about what is good for us. However, it is essential to remember that **most research is presented to the public through media or propagandists** with agendas. Tim offers guidelines for knowing which research is based on real science.

The Big Five
The Big Five are **tools most often used to exaggerate and brainwash**. It is essential to be able to spot them.

- Is a relative change (like percentages) being used to convince?
- Is this an observational study claiming to show cause and effect?

Observational studies cannot control or even document all of the variables involved.

- Does the study depend on self-recording or surveys?
- Is this diet study claiming to have a control group?
- Do the funders of the study have a vested interest in a particular outcome?

Other questions might include:

- When you ate the chicken or turkey, how often did you eat the skin?
- Did you usually choose dark meat, light meat, or both?

- How often do you eat a ½ cup amount of broccoli in the last three months?

Goal of This Chapter vs. the Goal of this Book
Tim states that the experiments in the book are flawed, especially since he was the single subject. However, this chapter is to help the reader look at published research and **not be tricked or misinformed**.

P-value: One Number to Understand
It is important to understand randomness and not be fooled by it. Three short stories illustrate **the importance of p-values, randomness, and statistical significance**.

Tools and Tricks
Tim provides a list of websites that address the chapter's concerns, such as biases, randomness, and skewing of reporting.

Spotting Bad Science 102

Dr. Ben Goldacre writes this chapter. His concern is how **experiment results can manipulate statistics** so that positive data overshadow negative results. Dr. Goldacre lists several ways that statistical analysis ensures positive trial results. These include ignoring the protocol entirely, playing with the baseline, ignoring dropouts, cleaning up the data, and being the best of five... no... seven, no... no... nine! They torture the data and try every button on the computer.

The Slow-Carb Diet - 194 People
The data was collected in questionnaires. 194 people responded to all the questions, and 58% indicated it was the first diet they could stick with. The data is provided.

(Potential) Weaknesses of the Data
Weaknesses in the methodology are:
- People could be making things up.
- This data set might not account for the dropouts - people who tried and gave up.

Discussion of Results
The conclusions did not reflect Tim's recommendations for using the Slow-Carb Diet.

These conclusions were: Eating just two meals a day, eating a vegetarian diet, counting calories, and skipping breakfast. It is impossible to determine cause and effect from the data collected. The next step would be testing the results with control and experimental groups.

Conclusion
The Slow-Carb Diet Works

Sex Machine II

Details and Dangers
Tim offers detailed protocols to help avoid problems, provide more background, and make the results more personalized.

- Protocol #1: Long-Term and Sustained. Tim gives detailed explanations and warnings concerning the supplements, vitamins, dosage, and methods needed to keep a long-term, sustained program. Tim includes the results he attained using Protocol #1.
- Protocol #2: Short-Term and Fun. This protocol is used the evening before the sex day. Tim breaks down a schedule and explains the different foods to consume.

Fixing One Problem, Causing Another: Deficiencies Created by Common Drugs and Training

Tim lists the techniques and drugs with their uses that can cause nutrient deficiencies.

The Meatless Machine I

Reasons to Try a Plant-Based Diet for Two Weeks

The Power of Positive Constraints
Limiting options is usually thought of as a bad thing, but in dieting, that is not necessarily true.

Moving From Ideal to Practical: Five Steps
A five-step sequence on eliminating and/or changing foods is given. Take them one step at a time.
>   Step 1. Remove starches.
>   Step 2. Ensure all meat is pasture-raised, grass-fed, or sourced within 50 miles.
>   Step 3: Eat meat only after 6:00 pm or only on the weekend or cheat days.

Step 4: Remove all meat except fish and/or eggs and dairy.

Step 5: Eat a 100% plant-based vegan diet.

Getting Organized

Tim answers these questions to be considered before beginning:

- How do I get enough protein on a vegan diet... without soy?
- What can I eat as a vegan while traveling?
  - Tim provides many profiles, menus, and recipes for a variety of vegan case studies.

The Meatless Machine II

John Berardi, Ph.D., a meat eater, designed a successful, almost 100% vegan diet for 28 days. The meal plan has been included.

When Scientists Become Guinea Pigs

Being the guinea pig allowed John to pinpoint and explain the non-obvious elements.

Questions for Dr. Berardi

Dr. Berardi answers the following questions about his diet.

- What was your daily macronutrient breakdown on this diet?
- What was your food cost for the week?
- What is your best estimate of your supplement cost per week?

- What do you think would have happened if you hadn't eaten eggs?
- If you'd continued the plant-based diet for six months, what do you think would have happened?
- Vegans talk about combining foods for complete proteins - rice and beans, for example, or legumes and seeds or nuts. What are your thoughts?
- Is it possible to be a vegan long-term, using only whole food and without protein supplements?
- What common mistakes do self-described "vegetarians" commit?
- What did you conclude after this experience?

Meat vs. Plant - Bridging the Divide

John's 28-day experiment was controversial to vegans and carnivores. He answers their concerns by stating that something can be learned from both.

Raw Food and Pottenger's Cats: Panacea or Misinterpreted Science?
Pottenger studied 900 cats over three generations to study the effects on the cats.

Experiment #1: Raw Meat vs. Cooked Meat.
Experiment #2: Raw Milk vs. Cooked Milk

Although Pottenger's findings found raw food to be better, Tim said that Pottenger did not know two things that impacted the findings: cats need taurine, and cats are carnivores.

Darwin's Rule - Eat for Fertility
After researching this book, Tim Ferriss has concluded that animal product is necessary for proper hormone production. Tim states that there is no sin in considering consuming animal products once a week if you are currently a vegan if it means you will be healthier.

Tools and Tricks
Tim provides a detailed list of websites about vegetarian and vegan diets.

Bonus Material
Tim lists several other materials to be used in conjunction with this book.

Key Points
- It is never too late to reinvent yourself.
- Research is sometimes presented to the public through the media or propagandists with an agenda. It cannot necessarily be trusted.
- Tim lists drugs and techniques that can cause nutrient deficiencies.
- To move to a meatless diet, follow a slow progression of food changes and removals.
- Tim states to follow Darwin's rule - Eat for fertility.

Action Plan

- Take inventory of all the things in the physical realm you've resigned to do poorly.
- Ask yourself, "If I could not fail, what would I want to do exceptionally?"
- Make some choices.
- What you choose can be a blueprint for not just a new body but a new life.
- Learn to tell if the information you are reading is based on science.
- If you decide to eat a diet with less meat, be sure to progress slowly.

_____

_____

_____

_____

_____

_____

_____

Thank You

We hope this book was meaningful and helpful to you!

We always strive to deliver to you the best books possible.

We are so appreciative and would like to thank you for

supporting us by reading until the very end.

Before you go, would you mind leaving us a review on

Amazon using the **QR code below**?

It will mean so much to us and encourage us to continue

creating the highest quality guides for you in the future.

Kindly,

The Knowledge Press Team